TEN LET

A Ron

P.E. Daunt

edited by Will Daunt

BournBridgeBooks

The main text for *Ten Letters to a Grandson* is © The Estate of P.E. Daunt 2019.

The photographs and 'Notes on the Text' are © Will Daunt 2019.

© **BournBridgeBooks** 2019, ISBN 9780244831196

Second impression, February 2020

BournBridgeBooks is a small and not-for-profit publishing enterprise based in Ormskirk, Lancashire. Books are sold at cost price and any incidental proceeds are donated to St. Mary's Church, Little Abington, Cambridgeshire, where P.E. Daunt completed two stints as church warden.

Contents

Introduction		6
Members of the family of Lucius Rutilius Rufus		9

The Letters

1	Priene, March	11
2	Priene, April	20
3	Pergamum, May	30
4	Priene, June	41
5	Mycale, July	52
6	Hierapolis and Aphrodisias, August	62
7	Priene, September	72
8	Karpathos, October	76
9	Karpathos and Knidos, November	86
10	Priene, December	97

Epilogue Athens, January	105
Geographical Names and Terms	116
Guide to Classical Names, Terms and References	119
A Note on the Text	124

" ... I gave up trying to be an atheist, something I was no good at."

P.E. Daunt, 2000

TEN LETTERS TO A GRANDSON

A Roman Following Christ

...as it might have been ...

By way of Introduction

For permission to publish this first translation of the Letters of Lucius Rutilius Rufus I am indebted to my friend and collaborator Professor Radu Mironescu, head of the Department of Greek within the Faculty of Letters of the ancient city of Cluj in Transylvania.

The general reader may not be aware of the sensation which the discovery of these letters three years ago created within the academic world, above all among scholars of the history of the reign of the Emperor Constantine and of the Christian Church at that time.

The text of the ten letters, of the very existence of which nothing was known, was discovered by a student of Mironescu who was examining the contents of a small but ancient library in the Moldavian monastery at Voronets. The letters were found as a kind of annex to a copy of that already well known Treatise on the Sublime which is attributed to Longinus. The manuscript of the Treatise can be ascribed to the eleventh or twelfth centuries, somewhat later than the Paris Codex 2036, the oldest known version of the Treatise; the text of the Letters appears to be of the same date and even from the same hand.

The Letters, of which there are ten (nine in Greek and one in Latin), purport to have been written by an elderly Roman landowner living in the Province of Asia (now western Turkey) at the end of the first quarter of the fourth century A.D. None of the scholars who have so far seen them has had any reason to doubt their authenticity on stylistic, historical or palaeographic grounds. An eleventh letter, addressed to the author of the first ten, is also thought to be genuine.

Professor Mironescu's *editio princeps* of the Letters will be published in the next eighteen months; the introduction and commentary will be both in English and Romanian. Meanwhile, in response to numerous requests, he has generously consented to this advance publication of a version of the Letters in English, and entrusted to me the tasks of translation, subject of course to his supervision, and publication. We have also agreed on the title *Ten Letters To A Grandson*, and that any profits from the present venture will be devoted to the further research on the Letters and their author.

A full description of the Letters, their author, their context and their significance must naturally await Mironescu's great work. I shall add here, with his permission, only a few points in support of the reader's understanding and enjoyment of the text, which to a large extent has the merit of speaking for itself.

The Letters are presented as having been written over a period of ten months, one each month from March to December. The year can with certainty be established as 324 AD: the Emperor Constantine has recently won his final victories over his rival Licinius (323; Letter 1), and is contemplating (Letter 4) the institution of the Ecumenical Council which took place in Nicaea in 325.

The author of the ten letters, Lucius Rutilius Rufus, is a man of substance living with the women of his family in a villa near Priene, on the coast of Asia Minor (now Turkey). He celebrates his seventieth birthday during the year of the Letters (Letter 5). He has retired from the imperial service, having reached the position of governor of a group of seven provinces comprising the imperial diocese of southern Gaul (Letter 9); as such he will have been a member of the equestrian order, the second in the hierarchy of Roman classes. His three sons and one son-in-law are distant from the family, engaged in the imperial service in various quarters of the Empire. For the convenience of the reader, a brief note of the members of the family mentioned in the Letters is given after this Introduction.

As a young man Lucius received what we should call a classical education. His principal interests are politics, literature and philosophy; he is also an amateur botanist.

The recipient of all the Letters is the author's grandson, another Lucius, who is spending the year in Athens enhancing his education. For this purpose the grandson is staying in the house of an Athenian, Hermogenes, who half a century before had been the close friend and fellow student of the grandfather. Hermogenes himself, being a professional rhetorician (approximately, professor of literature), appears to have acted throughout the year as the young man's moral and academic tutor as well as his host. He may have been the grandson of a Hermogenes who was an influential though pedestrian academic practising in Athens in the third century.

There is little doubt that the elder Lucius kept his own copies of the Letters, edited them and had them copied for distribution at least among his family and closest friends. The fact that no previous copy of them has come to light in modern times suggests on the other hand that he did not make them available to professional copyists for public distribution through booksellers.

The eleventh letter, appended here as an Epilogue, was written by Hermogenes in Athens and sent to the elder Lucius in the January of the same year (the New Year was not until March). It is possible that Lucius was so pleased with it that he decided to add it to his own ten, judging that it would enhance, rather than diminish, both the quality of the content and the literary unity of his own little work. An attractive alternative is that our manuscript is directly derived from Hermogenes's copy of the ten letters, to which he added his own copy of his January letter to Lucius without the latter's knowledge.

Nothing, I should perhaps add, is known of the author or his family beyond what we can learn from the Letters themselves. Of their future all we can say is that the family name does not appear among those of the landowners within the Asian provinces in any indexed text of the Byzantine period.

I must warn the reader that in my translation consistency in the spelling of the names and places has often had to be sacrificed in order to avoid pedantry.

P.E. Daunt   September 1996

Members and associates of the family of Lucius Rutilius Rufus

The Older Generations

Aulus I - father of the author.
Lucius I - the author of the Letters.
Helvidia - his wife.
Mango - Lucius' slave, married to Samia.
Aulus II - the author's unmarried brother, living in Pergamum.

The Family of Aulus III

Aulus III - eldest son of the author and Helvidia, in the imperial civil service in the province of New Dacia.
Caelia - his wife.
Lucius III - recipient of the Letters; only son of Aulus III and Caelia and only grandson of the author. Staying in Athens with Hermogenes and his granddaughter, Myrta, accompanied by his slave, Thrax.
Lucilla - elder daughter of Aulus III and Caelia, and elder sister of the recipient.
Aulia - her sister; younger daughter of Aulus III and Caelia and younger sister of the recipient.

The Family of Lucia

Lucia - married daughter of the author and Helvidia.
Quintus - her husband, in the imperial service in the province of Gallaecia.
Quintilla - elder daughter of Lucia and Quintus and elder cousin of the recipient.
Marcia - younger daughter of Lucia and Quintus and younger cousin of the recipient.

The Unmarried Sons of the Author

Lucius II - second son of the author and Helvidia, on the staff of the Caesar Crispus.
Gaius - youngest son of the author and Helvidia, in the imperial military service on the Persian frontier.

1. PRIENE, March.

By the time this letter comes to you, you will be past the stage of not knowing where you are or who anyone is, and may even have begun to be used to seeing the Acropolis from almost every point you may find yourself. Already the warmth of the welcome I am sure you had from Hermogenes and his granddaughter will have settled into familiarity, the ease of which will be ensured by the courtesy and thoughtfulness which will always (I am sure) inform your behaviour. The granddaughter is, I'm afraid, too young to be an interesting companion for you, but no doubt you will make friends among your fellow students in the Schools.

Before you left us, I promised to set down in writing what I *said* to you about the purpose of this year you are spending in Athens. My hope is that it will prove not of course the final climax of your education - something which will continue throughout your life - but nonetheless one of the most fruitful of all the stages in it. You will find that Hermogenes has a lot more to offer than the skills of a good scholar, though he has those in abundance; when we were fellow students he showed more originality of mind and a sharper critical eye than any of us.

While it is true that we are most happy when we are not conscious of our happiness, yet the quality of that experience, as of all experience, depends on those moments of reflection when we are conscious of ourselves and aware of our position as men among other men. Not to have a coherent and expressible philosophy of life is to be less than a man. The aim of civilisation is not to be ruled by philosopher kings in the Platonic style but to create a society in which all men and women are philosophers. This is not an endeavour in which we can see much recent progress, I fear; yet even in these times we who are Romans can perceive the difference between our moral and intellectual levels and those of the barbarians who surround our Empire.

I need hardly tell you that awareness of human reality, of what it is to be a man, begins with Homer. You remember how Alexander, having captured the treasure chest of the Great King, found that his Homer was the only thing he possessed worth keeping in it. I am too old to want to read and reread the Iliad; I have been through all that, it is (you might say) part of my mental luggage. I do not need to bring the direct experience of it back to life again. Since it is natural to look for some contrast between our daily reality and our books, one needs at my age to read of adventure, of magic and charm, of youthful vitality, of happy homecomings, of banquets rather than battles. So it is the Odyssey I turn to both for inspiration and for entertainment. With you no doubt it is the contrary: you are too young and so too serious to enjoy the Odyssey, which will seem to you trivial, women's stuff; you are now just the right age for the Iliad, ready to feel its pain deep in your bones and to learn from that both the truth of our human condition and the dependence of our soul's well being on poetry. One of the truths the Iliad tells us about our humanity is that there is only one difference that matters between men and gods, which is that men die and gods do not. The paradox is that this defect of mortality is the foundation of our dignity as men, the source of all our rights, the reason why the gods owe us not only compassion but also respect and honour.

Since death is our birthright, and we have so little time, the proof that a man recognises his own humanity lies in his design of a life which makes some kind of sense, which expresses a conscious pursuit of certain joys and a deliberate allegiance to certain principles. At seventeen, you are perfectly placed in life to understand this totally, since you are so much more sensitive to the reality of death and the brevity of life than you will be at thirty, say, or forty.

Of course I do not mean that you will establish your philosophy within one year, even a year spent in the 'city crowned with violets'. Some people are able to do this, I know; they can sit at the feet of a professional teacher for a few months, pay him his fee and come away bearing a neat packet of doctrines, much as a man may buy a cloak in a shop. But from what I know of you, that is not for you a possible choice. You will want to find you own road even if it takes all your life to do this, as it has taken and is taking mine.

During this year you will have many occasions to reflect on what since your early boyhood I have told you are the two most enlightening maxims of the humane philosophy, the dictum of Protagoras and that of Terence.

It is worth remembering their different provenances. When Protagoras announced that "Man is the Measure of all things" he was consciously aiming to emulate the brevity which he found to be admired in the tradition: the 'Know Thyself' and 'Nothing in Excess' of Apollo's Delphic professionals, The "Everything is in flux" of Heraclitus of Ephesos. He was speaking with his smart fee-paying clients in mind and intending to say something which was, if nothing else, patently clever. You will want to think carefully during your studies about the implication of the Protagorean maxim. For me, it represents not the epitome of humane philosophy but the ultimate travesty of it. If all judgment of what is good and bad, true and false, ugly and beautiful, lies with us mortal men alone, then we are on a slope down which we are likely to slide into the belief that convention is the only standard of behaviour; that belief in its turn may well lead us to the position which Plato put into the mouth of Thrasymachus in the Republic, that justice is no more than a pretty name we give to the advantage of the stronger.

If we are right in believing that the gods owe us honour, we may have to accept the consequence that we are only to have honour if there are gods to honour us.

You will come to your own conclusions on these matters as you compose your set pieces in answer to the questions which Hermogenes will surely pose you: Are the gods subject to fate, as Zeus was when the downfall of Troy was finally determined? Are the actions of the gods good because the gods perform them or do the gods perform them because they are good? At all events there are two conclusions which you will not be able to evade. The first is that the cynical and the sentimental views of all that we men have ever done are equally false, as a simple point of fact: the reality is the pattern of light and shade that I have always presented to you. The second is that we can never finally refute a sceptical view of the world, one that denies that the kosmos and we men in it have any final purpose and even rejects the very existence of the gods. In the end what we all have to do is to choose the path of scepticism or of believing, and follow wherever the path we have chosen leads us - unless, that is, we choose not to choose and so to live from day to day a life which excludes progress (since there is no path down which to go), a life without a philosophy, little better than that of the beasts.

"I am a man: I count nothing human alien from me."

Terence's pleasing declaration, known to every schoolboy, has all the urbanity typical of the comedy of manners from which it comes, does it not? I have no doubt you will think no worse of it for that: you have not gone to Athens from this little township to play the country bumpkin. And it is indeed true that if we use this as a precept and follow it, it will lead us in a good direction - as far as it goes. Let us examine what the precept can do for us, and what it cannot do.

Human sympathy for all mankind, without distinction of race or class, is essential to the imperial vision. Whenever we read the great historians, Thucydides, Polybius, Livy, Tacitus, we feel ourselves part of the triumphs and wretchednesses which they record and which have formed the good and evil of human activity at all times and in all climes. Heard and seen in the theatre or read in the privacy of the study, the works of the Greek tragedians move us profoundly because we feel ourselves engaged in the action and the passion of the drama; above all we admire the tragic hero, can imagine ourselves in his role and suffer with him in his downfall. Great paintings and sculptures move us almost to adoration not only in their glorification of the human form but also by allowing us to share the joy and wonder of the artist who created them.

For you it will not be a cause for severe distress that all these glories belong so irretrievably to the past, many of them to a past distant by over five hundred years. The kind of melancholy which finds pleasure in a gentle indulgence of itself is generally congenial to anyone at the threshold of adult life: having no significant past of his own to regret the passing of, a young man can afford to mourn the death of earlier cultures and can even find a kind of sad delight in the recognition of present decline; meanwhile the future, of which he has the promise of so much, is of little interest to him, since it can be trusted to look after itself. But for old men like me it is quite the contrary. There is no pleasure to be had from the knowledge that we must depend almost entirely on a distant past for our experience of great poetry and art; the best of what we can do now is to imitate former styles and achievements - for the rest we are relegated to the role of spectators and commentators. What is more, we are not insensitive to the futility of what we do, since the content no longer corresponds to reality and the vitality of the original is simply not there. To compensate me for the disillusionment of all that, the future, of which I can look forward to so little, is of the greatest possible importance and interest to me.

So, I ask myself, will there one day be a revival of the greatness of the past, anything to bear comparison with Periclean Athens or Augustan Rome? It seems to me at least a possibility. No one with any sense in them could take seriously the old tales of gold and silver ages, and so forth. Yet we know for sure that the times which Homer describes were heroic in some sense or another, and that what followed was a harder and leaner age out of which came the new and greater achievements in which the cities the remains of which lie around me as I write played so great a part. This would suggest that a decline may be succeeded by an ascent to previously unknown heights.

We know little of how men lived in the distant past, but this little is enough for us to draw important conclusions from it. There was a time when the use of iron was not known; and it is easy to guess, from the sherds we find in our fields and among old ruins, that there were days when pottery was far less well made and decorated than when Exekias was potting and painting in Athens, or even than the inferior commercial products of our own time. Old history books which tell us the stories of how Carthage was founded by the Phoenicians, and the cities of Sicily, south Italy and southern Gaul by the Greeks (some of them departing from these very shores) prove to us that there was an age when there were no civilised people living west of Italy. Even clearer is what travellers can tell about the lives of people living even now beyond the frontiers of our Empire and untouched by the kingdoms of the east. We know that such people find all their food by hunting, that they live in mean and fragile huts and that they go about clothed in the rough skins of animals. We Romans now are far behind the best of the Greeks in art, literature and freedom, but in many practical ways we are more prosperous than they were, and in all respects far less behind them than we are in advance of the barbarians of Africa and Scythia, of Caledonia or Marcomannia.

It follows, surely, that even if we - I mean we, the human race - may suffer setbacks, experiencing bad times as well as good, yet our story is one of progress. If that is true of the past, then it must at least be possible for the future, indeed more likely than not. Naturally, we cannot know when the next big step forward will be. If we were to ask the opinion of the good citizens of Priene, or even of their more sophisticated neighbours of Miletos or Ephesos, we know very well what their answer would be: the good times are only a year or two away, and the proof of this is the series of great victories that Constantine has won over Licinius.

Good as is the prospect of an Empire truly united again after so many years of perilous fragmentation, I fear that I cannot share that optimism. For sure, there is no prospect of good times immediately ahead as far as the arts and literature are concerned. In a year or two, whatever the good ladies of our family have to say about it, you will be old enough for your first visit to Rome. You will see the proof of what I say, as I saw it during my stay there two years ago, displayed before the eyes of the world in the decoration of the great Arch of Constantine by the Colosseum; it had been dedicated a few months before my arrival in the Eternal City. The low reliefs on the attic and in the roundels in the middle range of decoration were done some two hundred years or so ago: they still demonstrate all the elegance and dignity of the great tradition; they are truly imperial, Roman, not Greek, it is true, but within one and the same civilisation, worthy of the great originals which inspired them. Below are friezes of our own time, purporting to show our Supreme Augustus in all his splendour, formally presenting himself to the world in the presence of his court of great men and elders. You cannot imagine anything meaner or more pitiable than these wretched misrepresentations, anything more barbarous simply. By this criterion, all the human artistic endeavour since the very first Olympiad was celebrated has ended in failure.

It is not enough simply to observe the dispiriting contrasts exposed on that monument: we must try to understand why it is so. In doing so we shall come to the heart of the reason why it would be vain to hope for any great change in the quality of our civilisation simply as a result of Constantine's supremacy, however benevolent and enlightened he may prove to be once unchallenged. Our literary and artistic inadequacies cannot be attributed to lack of knowledge or of skill, still less to lack of wealth or other resources; they are more like what our physicians like to call a symptom than the disease itself. We cannot do these things well because we do not have the heart for it. It is a problem of the human spirit, and in particular one to do with freedom.

In the domain of literature there is a decadence which seems to follow inevitably from a loss of political freedom and vigour. I have no doubt that Hermogenes will be asking you to reflect on the difference between the diverse and vibrant humanity of Aristophanes and the cultured uniformity of Menander's mannered comedies. Further on in its downward career, this decline is precisely depicted in the Treatise on the Sublime, which our professor Longinus made the basis of all his teaching when Hermogenes and I studied together in Athens fifty years and more ago. (Many of his pupils supposed Longinus had composed it himself, though he never claimed this). Mango has found the passage for me:

"Are we then to believe in that familiar opinion, that democracy is a good nurse of men of genius, and that generally speaking outstanding writers flourished only under democracy and died out with it? It is freedom, according to this view, which has the ability to cherish the minds of noble men and give them hope... But we who live now seem to have been brought up from childhood in equitable slavery, swaddled as it were from the time of our first tender awareness in the habits and behaviour of slaves. We have never tasted that most lovely and fruitful source of literature, I mean freedom, and so we emerge with a talent for absolutely nothing except flattery .... As we read in Homer, 'The day of enslavement takes away half our manly virtue'".

This is a topic which I could not bear to think of you overlooking in your studies while you are in Athens, of all cities in the world. And it is too big a one for me to address in what is already in danger of becoming too long a letter; it must wait for another time.

Meanwhile, we should be grateful for the inclusiveness and generosity of Terence's few words. By encouraging us to consider the whole picture of human endeavour with sympathy, they help us to see the broad pattern of man's progress and so rescue us from the pessimism of the cynics. Yet, for all the good directions in which Terence may lead us, we shall need other guides if we are to acquire a philosophy which is more than merely comfortable and tolerant. As you make progress in your studies of logic in the months ahead, you will often come across the distinction between what is essential and what is sufficient. I leave you with the thought that a humane philosophy in the Terentian style is the one without being the other.

I have not forgotten that third most famous of the maxims of humanism, Seneca's "To mankind, mankind is holy". In this connection, you will I hope be amused rather than shocked to hear that when I make my regular visit to Miletos I have taken to calling on Philip, the Christian bishop there. We share a glass or two of wine - not a wine I should normally drink, it must be said - and talk about old gods and new. He has great hopes of Constantine; there are rumours not only of imperial conversion but of a new policy which would go well beyond toleration, affording Christianity the imperial blessing, even some kind of official status. We can forgive the glint in the bishop's eyes when he speaks of this: it was not so long ago that he was in hiding, lucky to escape the obscene death inflicted on so many of his co-religionists during Diocletian's persecutions. Imagine too the prospect, not only of peace and honour but of power and wealth! Do not, I beg of you, accuse me of sycophancy. My attention to this so ambiguous religion is a perfectly genuine and disinterested one. I can see advantages in the generalisation of one unifying cult throughout the Empire (and if any, why not this one?), although there could be grave dangers in that too. Anyway, even if the bishop and his fellows see all their hopes brought to fulfilment, I can hardly imagine myself threatened with persecution for not worshipping the gentle Galilean.

There are, I must confess, some phrases the bishop uses, often words which he claims to have been spoken by 'the Christ' himself, which affect me in a strange way, not quite like anything else I have come across in my reading or conversation; they have too a way of sticking in my memory, and of returning to my conscious mind as it were unbidden. There is something here which I feel bound to explore further: a man in retirement has plenty of time on his hands. I have persuaded the bishop to let Mango copy some of the sacred texts of his faith for me. He was reluctant to agree to that; this surprised me until I remembered how characteristic it is of all priesthoods to protect the element of mystery in their cults and to hold their uneducated worshippers in awe by keeping sacred objects, including texts, strictly to themselves. In the end he has only agreed on the condition of my promise that the copies will be for the use of myself and my immediate family only. I was besides able to offer an inducement, by proposing to contribute to the cost of the bishop's project to have all his holy texts copied onto vellum. It is high time: his papyrus rolls are ancient and much used. Mango will have to handle them with care, or whole sections will fall apart in his hands.

Together with this you will have found letters from all the ladies of this house, all seven of them. No doubt those of your sisters and cousins are full of nonsense, and those of your grandmother, mother and aunt Lucia full of admonitions about not catching cold and the importance of good regular meals - not a facility likely to be lacking in the house of Hermogenes. The girls are constantly speculating about the risk you run of falling into the snares of wicked women. Their aim is to provoke from me comment just indelicate enough to raise your grandmother's eyebrow without exciting an outright rebuke. They are generally successful.

Spring is now well advanced, a little ahead no doubt of what you are finding in Attica. All over our beloved headland the planes and wild figs are in full leaf, and already even the chestnuts at the tops of the gorges are showing plenty of green. It is this contrast of the bright colours of the broad-leaved trees with the sombre hues of our sea-pines, cypresses, wild olives and evergreen oaks among them which gives the vegetation of Mycale its particular charm. Underneath the trees the green and purple hellebores are in full flower, and by following my favourite tracks I can easily reach the stations of the white ones high among the crags. On this side of the hills, where the village goats have devoured all but the toughest low shrubs, a few orchids are already in bloom, but it is too early to let the girls loose on them with their note-tablets.

Mango sends his fond regards to your Thrax, who I am sure is looking after you dutifully. We are all well here, and glad to see the end of the cold winds and long nights of winter. Do not be alarmed at the letter I am sending to your revered host with this: I am encouraging him to foster your freedoms rather than constrain them.

2. PRIENE, April

I was amused to hear that Hermogenes has been teasing you about the backwater in which we have chosen to live, and asking why, if I had to settle among the barbarians of Asia, I could not have chosen Ephesos, or even better Pergamum, where there are at least libraries designed to serve the needs of a man of scholarly habits.

Tell him from me that I am not so isolated from the benefits of civilisation as he supposes. Is his geography so poor that he does not know that I can reach Ephesos in a day? And has he forgotten that your great uncle Aulus lives in Pergamum, so that I can stay there as my brother's guest whenever I like?

You may tell him too that when I retired from the imperial service I had three solid reasons for choosing to buy this villa and estate so close to Priene.

The first consideration was that of safety for myself and my family. Now that the good Maeander river has filled most of the Bay of Latmos with silt, Priene is no longer accessible to sea-raiders as it once was, while on the land side it sits safely apart from the main north and south road which passes from Miletos to Ephesos. Since it is many years since Priene enjoyed the wealth of a busy port, there would be little inducement for looting armies to make the detour. And if the worst were to happen, we have the thickets and forest of the headland behind us, with pathways known only to us and a few local hunters. I do not need to remind you of the special provisions we have made in case we have to resort to the wilds of Mycale until some storm of invasion blows over.

My second reason was quite simply the charm and beauty of the place. How right old Herodotus was to praise the climate of Ionia, the 'golden mean' between the damp and cold further north and the heat and drought of the south! And of all Ionia, I have heard of nowhere to compare with our headland of Mycale. We have hunting in the autumn, unlimited fuel for the winter, shade to cool us and incomparably clear sea to swim in throughout the summer. And all the spring, on into early summer and again when the first rains of autumn come, we have a profusion and variety of wild flowers almost equal to Rhodes, Karpathos or Crete. My book on the Plants of Mycale is making good progress by the way, and I have hopes of completing it next winter. It is natural that botanical writing has been dominated for centuries by the herbalists; but I want to revive the purely scientific approach of the great Theophrastus. Perhaps my book will shame at least one or two of our poets into behaving more like Virgil instead of rhapsodising flowers without knowing one single plant from another. Your sister Lucilla has promised to do the drawings for me and has already come up with some good examples; her little cousin Marcia is beginning to show some of the same talent too.

And my third reason was a wish, a whim if you like, to end my days in that part of the whole world where freedom all began. That brings me to the promise in my last letter to explain how I think that certain of the greatest human achievements are linked to political freedom and depend on it.

I hope Hermogenes would not be offended if he knew of my insistence that it was not in Athens that political freedom was invented. Certainly, it was there that, for better and for worse, Greek democracy saw its richest flowering. But it was in this region that the idea of the people as sovereign, and indeed the whole vision of a single city as an autonomous state, were first conceived and developed. It is not difficult to guess how and why this happened. As we have seen so often in the assaults of the last two hundred years on the frontiers of our Empire, great movements of people normally take place over land. Exceptionally, uniquely for all we know, the Greeks who came down into Greece from the north, and then found too little room for them all to live in among the narrow valleys and rocky ranges of that country, got themselves into ships and swept back east over the Aegean Sea. They arrived here on the coast of Asia, as they did among the islands, in small groups, closely united by a common bond of loyalty after overcoming together the various perils of the sea, and so sharing a strong sense of equal membership in the little communities which they proceeded to set up. Especially here on the coastal strip of Asia, that sense of community and equality would have been reinforced by the struggle to establish and maintain themselves against the opposition of the local tribes already living here.

I know that your pedagogues have taught you to believe that the greatest tribute to democracy in the whole of literature is the Funeral Speech of Pericles, as it is recorded by Thucydides; no doubt they made you learn by heart the passages about freedom and tolerance and versatility, and the call to the Athenians to fall in love with their city. But for me the true foundation text of democracy is not that but something far older and from this coast:

>A tiny rock-built citadel
>(This also said Phocylides)
>Is finer far, if ordered well,
>Than all your frantic Ninevehs.

Phocylides wrote in Miletos, the outline of which I can see across the silt fields and salt flats from my chamber window as I sit here dictating to my loyal Mango.

You must not undervalue the wonder of what Phocylides wrote or of the reality which he expressed. All the known examples of high and vigorous civilisation - Egypt, Assyria, Babylon, Media, Persia, Lydia - had one salient feature in common, the hereditary autocracies to which they were without exception and at all times subject; I am reminded of the chamber at Elephantine which Herodotus admired and which the Pharaoh Amasis had made out of a single block of stone: these great monarchies were monolithic, the power of the ruler was absolute. And apart from them there was nothing, nothing other than the barbaric tribes of the south, west and north. As a rule in history we find new institutions and systems of government appearing as developments out of ones that exist already: only in the case of the invention of the city state, and with the notion of the sovereign citizens making their own laws, do we find something completely new which seems to owe nothing to the tradition.

It is little wonder that having created freedom the Ionians felt for it a passionate devotion unlike any feelings perceptible in other cultures. Indeed, this political passion was quite unintelligible to non-Greeks in ancient times: Plato tells the story of the Egyptian sage who finds no explanation for the way Greeks behave and has to rid himself of the problem by a witty dismissal of it: "You Greeks are always children".

The ardour of this Ionian love of one's city is well

illustrated by the story of the men of Phocaea (not much left of that city now, I'm afraid). After the capture of the city by the forces of the Great King and its subjection to the Persian satrap, the citizens of Phocaea were faced with a terrible dilemma: which was the worse course, to leave the city they loved or remain there as wretched subjects of a regime they detested? Some of them chose the former way. But the choice was so painful, and the need to reinforce their commitment so desperate, that they took with them as they set sail (they knew not whither) a large lump of lead; once in deep water they heaved this over the side and all swore a great oath they would not betray the endeavour by returning to their city until the lump of lead rose to the surface of the sea. But that night as they lay moored in a bay, they were overcome by "longing and compassion" for their city; and so next day they abjured their oath and went home. To understand the power of their emotion we must appreciate its reciprocal quality: they longed for their city because they needed it; they felt compassion for their city because they knew it needed them.

Passion and loyalty such as these generated a degree of energy and vitality the like of which is not known to us from the records of any other time or place. You know well enough already how it was in these cities here that philosophy and the theoretical vision of mathematics and science were invented, where much of the first great lyric and elegiac poetry was written and many of the first great Greek buildings conceived and erected. And you know how it was from here that many of the most adventurous trading and colonising enterprises set out, reaching far into the Black Sea, to Egypt, to Sicily and southern Italy, and even into the Carthaginian preserves of southern Gaul, Corsica and Spain.

It must have seemed that there could be no limit to the triumphs of the human spirit which the citizens of these cities would achieve as if it were as of right. You must however found your own political education on a full understanding of the two destructive forces which affected the city states like diseases and made their downfall and the loss of their precious freedoms inevitable.

The first of these was the rivalry between them which made them generally incapable of uniting against a common foe. It was not that no efforts for unity were ever made, or that no successes of unity ever recorded. This very headland on which we live affords double testimony to what has been attempted in a spirit of cooperation. The first instance is one you will come across in your studies of Herodotus and the other authors of the Persian Wars. It was here on Cape Mycale that the Athenians with the Spartans and their Dorian allies caught the Persian fleet beached on the southern shore not far from the ruins of the Temple of Demeter which we know; they stormed the palisade that defended the ships and destroyed them all. The Ionians compelled as subjects to serve in the Persian ranks deserted during the battle; especially the men of Miletos, posted to guard the pathways through the heights of the headland in the event of a Persian retreat, turned against their masters and led them back to where the victorious Greeks could complete their slaughter. This was a conclusive victory and the whole seaboard was liberated from the barbarian. But it was also the last time that the leading free Greek cities ever collaborated against a common foe.

The second cooperative instance is one well enough known to you, since it is only a year or so ago that I took you with me to a meeting of the town councillors of the Ionian Dodecapolis at the Panionium sanctuary on the north side of the neck of our Mycale. What you saw there was as you realised little more than traditional ceremonial; one can hardly expect a ritual sacrifice to Poseidon to mean now what it did when the cities taking part were nautical masters of the Aegean, Euxine and Ionian seas. Nor was the business to be done, the settlement of minor boundary disputes, the quarrels over the upkeep of roads and the hair-splitting over the dates of local festivals, at anything like the level of debate which this lovely, cistus-loving hillside had seen in the distant past. Yet there is some glory in the fact that the fathers of these cities have been meeting here together for nearly one thousand years, and in the knowledge that here was launched the first organised attempt to ensure cooperation between free cities, and so to gain the best of both worlds of autonomy and mutual support. The semicircle of eleven rows of marble seats is still as it has been for centuries, and so are the thrones of the Presidency, together with the tradition that they should always be occupied by men in whose territory the sanctuary and meeting place lie, our own dear folk of Priene.

It was here the old Ionians conspired their own first brave attempt to rebel from the Persian overlords, and here they agreed that Dionysius of Phocaea should be the admiral of their combined fleet, surely then rivals with the Athenians for the best fighting navy in the world. Yet as I look across to the south, a little to the right of my view of Miletos, I can see rising from the silt plain the hump of what was once the island of Lade, off which the fatal battle was fought. You remember the discontent with the leadership, the plotting of puppet dictators against the revolt, the desertion of the men of Sames, the shameful defeat at sea, the collapse of the uprising, the destruction of Miletos; the Milesians had brought eighty ships to that day, to our little Priene's twelve. Lade stands for us as the model of all the collaborative failures which were to haunt the Greeks down the years and ensure the final loss of their liberties.

Even more important for your political education is an understanding of the second of the lethal disorders to afflict the free city states, that of political mania. You will read this year all that Plato and Aristotle have to say about the various forms of legitimate government, and will I do not doubt reach three conclusions. The first is that there is no theoretical answer to the question whether the best way to govern a free state is by means of the direct rule of a sovereign people or through the agency of a minority ruling class. And the second is that what matters most of all *is* the keeping of the conflict between the proponents of radical democracy and the champions of oligarchical regimes at a moderate and temperate level, since once the struggle becomes extreme legitimate government becomes impossible and power falls into the hands of one or another kind of tyrant; so freedom is lost, and the one outcome results which all the great writers agree is the most hateful. And your third conclusion, drawn as much from Roman as from Greek experience, will be that the polarisation of opinion between the popular party and their opponents, and so the escalation of the conflict between them, are inevitable: there is something in our human nature which leads us ineluctably to the loss of our freedom through our abuse of it. It is as if it were fated that Greek democracy should lead to Alexander and the Roman to Augustus.

All this was analysed with meticulous accuracy by

Thucydides, whom you will find to be the most formidable of all the Greek intellects. Do not complain because his analytical passages are so difficult to understand! The reason is that he is penetrating below the surface of events and for that purpose has to compel words and combinations of words to take on tasks which had literally never before been required even of the Greek tongue. If you are never to forget where the political madness of free, civilised people leads, you cannot do better than to keep before your mind the narrative passage - a much easier one! - in which the historian tells us of the conclusion of the civil war in Corcyra:

"When the Corcyreans of the popular party had their opponents as prisoners in their hands they shut them up in a large building, and afterwards took them out in batches of twenty at a time and made them pass between two lines of hoplites drawn up to form a lane along which the prisoners went bound together, and were beaten and stabbed by those between whom they passed when anyone saw a personal enemy among them. Men with whips went along with them to hurry on their way those who were going forward too slowly. About sixty men were taken out and killed in this way before the others in the building realised it; finally they became aware of what was happening and refused any more to go out of the building. The Corcyreans of the popular party got up on to the top of the building, demolished the roof, and hurled down tiles and shot arrows at the people below, who protected themselves as best they could, though in fact most of them now began to take their own lives by driving into their throats the arrows that were shot at them or by hanging themselves with cords taken from some beds that happened to be there or with strips made out of their own clothing. Night fell on the scene and for the great part of the night they were still doing themselves to death by all manner of means and being killed by the arrows of those on the roof. When it was day the Corcyreans of the popular party piled them up and bundled them on to waggons and took them outside the city. The women who had been captured were sold as slaves".

We know what barbarian invaders have done to Roman citizens, their wives and children, when they have plundered our cities and countryside. Yet Thucydidies is telling us of the behaviour of fellow citizens to each other, men who had worshipped in the same temples, neighbours perhaps whose children were lovers.

Rather than panic in the face of barbarian hordes, it is this insanity, as it was too in Rome when the blood in the forum had to be mopped up each morning, that has led to the surrender of freedoms to autocracy, to tyrants, dictators and monarchs and now to emperors. Whatever nostalgia we feel for the freedoms of the past, however much we deplore the monotony, inertia and deadly orthodoxy of imperial rule, we must admit that we have no experience or fear of scenes such as Thucydides describes. And now that religious toleration seems assured we shall be spared many of the revolting scenes in our theatres and amphitheatres which disgraced us during the persecutions.

Now indeed as the myriads of our enemies mass perpetually against us on our eastern frontiers, we have no choice. It is impossible to foresee any other future for your father's generation or even your own than that offered by a gigantic dictatorship of one or several military commanders. Men of our class will continue to do what I and my brother have done, what your father and uncles are doing, to serve the imperial security in the army or as civilians supporting the legions, for much of the time in one or another outpost of empire. In this way we can at least avoid the worst of that apathy towards everything but the mere pursuit of wealth and pleasure which the author of the Treatise on the Sublime I mentioned in my last letter perceived to be the curse of our culture ever since the fall of the Republic.

Meanwhile, it is this imperial military power that we must thank for the fact that we can travel to almost any corner of the civilised world in comparative security. At the same time we have to recognise that, as well as the permanent loss of our political freedom, there is another price to pay. As I warned you in my last letter, our literature and our practice of the arts will be, as far as can be predicted, at best a feeble imitation of the achievement of the past, and, at worst, doomed to show more and more the influence of the barbarian societies which surround and obsess us.

I have now in my happy possession Mango's copyings of four sections of the holy Christian writings which the Bishop Philip has kindly made available to me. They are, it seems, the most important of all the texts which make up the collection the bishop simply calls the Bible. They are called Evangels, since they bring the 'good news' of the life and teaching and death of Jesus the Christ; the Christians regard his death as well as his life as good news for reasons not quite clear to me yet. There are four different authors, all said to have been followers of Jesus. Of these, the fourth, John, is a deeper and more philosophical writer than the other three, one of whom however, called Luke, was, the bishop tells me, a physician and evidently an intellectual: although he tells the same story as the other two (named Matthew and Mark), he has some striking passages which are quite his own. The texts are all in their original language, a Greek quite easy to read; the style is generally acceptable, without solecisms or exaggerated effects, although it is naturally written in the vernacular not in the classical Attic manner. There is a puzzle here, since John at least of the four was according to the story a simple villager and lake fisherman. Perhaps what we have here is a cultivated version of a number of simpler texts or even of accounts passed on merely by word of mouth - or, of course, of a combination of these.

My new interest and acquisition has aroused considerable interest in the family. You can imagine the talk: "What is the old man up to now?" The girls have done everything even their lively imaginations could suggest to wheedle the truth out of Mango, who has enormously enjoyed his importance in defending the secret from their wiles. Naturally, I only allowed this to go on for a few days, as I have always intended to share this strangely appealing story and teaching with my ladies, and with the servants too. So we have adopted a new custom, one which we are already enjoying and which we all look forward to. After dinner we come together in the heat of the day under the big plane tree, and take it in turns to read passages aloud, Mango and his wife and any of the other servants who can read joining in.

We are all astonished at the force and beauty of many of the passages. It is hard to say which is more impressive, the life that this Christ lived or his teaching; most striking of all perhaps is the coherence which anyone can see between the two. At the same time, there are all sorts of complications and anomalies in the writings. That there are inconsistencies and contradictions in details of the narrative is inevitable, and does not in any way detract from the total validity or value of the group as a whole. What is more disturbing is the number of apparent contradictions in the teaching; this suggests to me that at some stage a true account of what this man had to say has been corrupted by an overlay of ideas quite at variance with his. I have gently put this possibility to the bishop but his reaction was so immediate and extreme, a combination of distress and anger, that I dropped the point at once and have made a resolve to be most cautious in this matter in the future.

At the heart of the problem is the evident contradiction (if that is what it is) between the vision of a gentle and loving god and that of a god who is censorious and irascible. There is of course a traditional explanation of this in the Olympian religion of our forefathers: the gods have moods, and these are apparent in nature, the sea being calm or savage because Poseidon has these changes of temper, and so with the weather and the sky-god Zeus. But, as you can imagine, the Epicurean in me - and it is there, though I would not like you to over-estimate its influence - wants to rebel at once from that. Must we not insist that the philosophers, whose reflections have been carrying us forward now for a thousand years, have taken us beyond that point, and made it impossible for us to go back to it? Are we really to worship a god who is more petulant, wilful and vindictive than we would expect a reasonably decent fellow citizen to be, let alone the virtuous man of the Stoics? What do you think, I wonder?

The barer parts of our nearby hillsides are now adorned with orchids in their thousands, and all the girls are busy recording. They will have to work hard and fast, as the season is so short and I am determined to have a complete record by the end of it this time. I already know there are seventeen kinds which I can distinguish with confidence, and have a good idea of how they are distributed over the area; but your cousin Quintilla, who regards herself as the real expert, is convinced that that there are over twenty. I both hope and expect she is right.

We are all glad to hear that your Greek studies are proceeding well, and that you are also finding time to get to know the architectural beauties of Athens. Do not neglect your Latin, however.

3 -PERGAMUM, May

I am dictating this letter in Latin, as I have been worrying that during your stay in Athens you will not make any further progress in the quality of your writing in that language, and may even regress. Please write in Latin too when you reply, so that I can be reassured you are not letting your Greek spoil your Latin style.

You will be surprised to see that I am sending this from Pergamum: it is not like me to leave my Mycale just as the sea is warm enough for swimming and the cistus is in all its beauty over the foothills.

The reason is that I had a few days ago a letter from your great-uncle Aulus, telling me that he was seriously ill and anxious about the outcome. So of course I came at once and have stayed with him while he has set about getting the better of a dangerous infection in the chest.

Inevitably we went to the celebrated Health Centre and shrine of Asclepius in the lower town here. I had not had occasion to visit it before, and have been quite astonished at its massive size and the bewildering number of patients (or worshippers, if you prefer) crowding round all the facilities there. My brother was anxious to make a sacrifice to the god, and I did not oppose this, although in my sceptical way I have no doubt that the only possible effect this can have is on the patient's morale. Since however improving how people feel about their condition may well be as important a part of the medical art as healing their physical symptoms, and since even Socrates at the moment of death not only remembered that he "owed a cock to Asclepius", but evidently wished his friends to discharge the vow, we should not I suppose be too proud in these matters.

Aulus insisted on taking the waters in the pump room, where the combination of the crowds and the heat was so oppressive that I doubt of his survival if we had not managed to get him away at the first opportunity. Fortunately he was too exhausted to prevent us bringing him home before he could be sold any of the outrageously expensive miracle drugs which the swarms of charlatans were trying to press on us.

Since then I have subjected my brother to my own medical

regime: plenty of red wine, salads well soaked in oil and garlic, days spent out of the heat of the sun, and as much rest and sleep as possible. The signs of recovery are already evident and in a few days I shall be able to leave him to the care of his faithful Getas and make my way home.

Although it is only early in the evening, Aulus is already sleeping deeply, with Getas to watch over him. So, I am free to sit on the porch, enjoy my wine and the soft evening sun and dictate this letter to you.

Certainly, I am entirely happy that you are discussing those parts of my letters which are not personal with Hermogenes - particularly if this inspires him to threaten you with compositions on themes such as the one you mention on "The more freedom, the less justice".

To understand justice you will need to study the fifth book of that version of Aristotle's Treatise on Ethics which was edited by his son, Nicomachus. You will miss the stylistic beauties of Plato, and may need to draw yourself a diagram or two in order to follow the good Stageirite when he moves into his technical vein on the subject of proportionality. But I believe you will agree that there is a lot of common sense in his analysis.

We need not detain ourselves over what Aristotle has to say about justice in the broad or general sense, meaning simply the whole of virtue as it is applied to our relations with other people.

More interesting is his vision of that branch of justice in its narrower, more specific, sense, which he calls "corrective". It is obvious that in any civilised society freedom has to be limited by laws which prevent people from practising violent or deceitful crimes against each other, and which require men to honour their contracts. There are two questions of outstanding general interest in this corrective domain. The first is whether such laws should, or should all, be applied to slaves. Obviously, a master is free to make a slave work against his will, and to move him from one place to another whatever his own wishes, and such compulsion is a sort of violence against the person which the law would not permit to be performed against a free citizen. But we can only welcome Constantine's recent decrees which protect slaves from much of the maltreatment and physical punishment to which they have been traditionally subject. This reform is true to the spirit of our times; it may indeed owe something to the influence which Christian philosophy has had on the Emperor. I have nothing but contempt for those of my more conservative contemporaries who deplore it as a sign of decadence. The regulation that in courts of law the evidence of a slave is only admissible if given under torture is a practice which has always disgusted me. The custom whereby if a slave kills his master all the slaves in that household are put to death is a further example of excessive brutality, and yet another is the execution of runaway or rebel slaves by means of crucifixion - the form of death, as it happens, inflicted on the Christians' prophet, as you may know.

You will never have seen your grandmother or me punishing a servant in any of the barbarous ways still practised in some respectable households. At first our reasons for abandoning these practices were rather aesthetic than ethical: we found such a crude exercise of power, and its aftermath, simply distasteful. Then, when we had children, we came to understand the degenerating moral effect that the use of physical punishment has on family life and very soon decided that it had no place in our domestic economy. Time has proved us right in practice: the absence of cruel punishment actually reduces the need for it, to the point where that need simply vanishes. So you have no reason to be surprised that our son and daughter have followed our example in your upbringing and that of your peers.

The second most important question in the realm of corrective justice is the extent to which restraining laws should be applied in the various situations which occur in war. Whereas physical violence against women and children is always condemned, the treatment of captured soldiers and of men generally is a disputed area. Do you think, for example, that Julius Caesar was justified in amputating the right hands of all the men whom he captured at Alesia, and whose rebellion he regarded as putting his whole conquest of Gaul at risk? And is the conqueror of a rebel city entitled to put the men of military age to death and sell the women and children into slavery?

The question brings us back to Thucydides. When the important city of Mytilene on Lesbos rebelled from Athens and was subjugated, exactly that punishment was at first voted against them and a trireme was sent across the Aegean to announce the sentence and see it carried out. Next day, after a great debate in the Assembly, the Athenian democracy repented of its severity, and sent the great State Galley in pursuit to cancel the command. Fortified with wine and barley supplied by the Mytilenean ambassadors, rowing continuously and taking it in turns to sleep, they arrived as the sentence of death and slavery was being promulgated and so just in time to prevent its execution. It is clear that, at least in Thucydides's view, it was Athenian honour which was saved that day quite as much as Mytilenean lives and freedoms: when a few years later, the island of Melos rebelled, the full horror of execution and enslavement, Greek against Greek, was exacted. The cynicism of the justifications which the historian attributes to the Athenians on that occasion shows that in his opinion Athens was from that moment morally doomed.

In warfare between different cultures on the other hand such scruples have not generally applied. It is ironical that it was Delos, the sacred island where the lovely Apollo and his mysterious twin sister Artemis were born, which flourished for centuries as the centre of the international slave trade - a trade that depended entirely on the ample supply of enslaved prisoners of war. The consul Tiberius Gracchus, father of the great tribune, captured so many slaves in his Sardinian campaign that he brought down the market and "cheap as a Sardinian" became a proverbial expression. In the great days of the Roman Republic, consuls over a number of years conducted against tribes in the north west of Italy campaigns which were little more than slave hunts. Many of these were worked in gangs on estates and in mines, suffering dreadful conditions: the censorious moralist Cato said it was cheaper to work them to death and replace them than to treat them well.

All that we can say, then, as far as concerns the application of the principle of corrective justice, is that the world does not seem to be getting totally worse, and, at least in respect of the treatment of slaves, is even getting better, actually more just.

Aristotle rightly distinguishes from corrective justice another kind which he calls distributive justice. By this he means the fairness with which the society distributes the good things of life among its citizens. The good things which he mentions are honour, money and safety; fairness is an example of his favourite notion of a 'golden mean' between too much of these and too little. I suppose we can take 'safety' in a rather broad sense as including comfort as well as personal security; or else we can include in 'money' all the good things which money can buy, good food, good clothes, warmth in winter, horses and so on. The Greek word he uses for 'fair' is 'isos' which of course also means 'equal'. But he very soon makes it clear that distributive justice does not require the giving of identical amounts of the good things to every one. The reason for this is that men are not equal. At this point we have to remember that all we are reading here is Nicomachus's writing up of the notes he took of his father's lectures. What we find is one of the most critical statements in all of moral philosophy given us in a mere handful of imprecise words; we are told that "everyone agrees that distributive justice must be based on some sort of principle of worth".

Immediately we are brought face to face with a stark reality: in practice this means that the implementation of distributive justice is entirely in the domain of factional politics. Again, we have to be content with a text which is little better than shorthand: in a democracy, the philosopher tells us, the criterion of worth is free birth, in a commercial or land-owning plutocracy it is wealth, in an hereditary aristocracy it is noble lineage. There is another category listed: in a pure aristocracy, the criterion would be virtue.

This brings us back to the cynical position which Plato in 'The Republic' attributes to the professional sophist Thrasymachus: that 'justice' is merely a fancy name which we give to what is in reality simply whatever is to the advantage of the stronger. And if we look at this from a theoretical point of view, we may easily come to the conclusion that he is right, since the notion of a pure aristocracy of the most virtuous men is merely an ideal, which never has been and never could be realised; in reality, a wide or narrow distribution of wealth and other goods depends entirely on whether a popular or oligarchic party is in power.

If on the other hand we look at this from a historical viewpoint we shall find that that is not what generally happens. Instead, until the evil effects of escalation can be seen, some kind of balance between the power of the few and the power of the many is generally found, most successfully no doubt where this is a balance of political power established by means of a mixed constitution, of the kind Polybius (a historian you will not be expected to study this year) found in the best days of the Roman Republic.

So it comes about that the wealth of the rich can be not only reduced but put to the public good by means of tribute or taxes; poor peasants can be protected by law from the loss of their land through debt, and large estates can even be bought up compulsorily by the state for redistribution; the urban poor can be maintained by means of payment for public service as in ancient Athens or of doles as in Rome; the wages of workers can be adjusted up or down; common people can be endowed with land and other goods as a reward for military service.

Although slaves have generally come off badly in the operation of distributive as well as of corrective justice, the possibilities for them to accumulate money or other property and to undertake marriages which are accorded official recognition have been improving rather than declining since the start of our imperial period some three hundred and fifty years ago. Not only too are more slaves manumitted, but the opportunities for freedmen to prosper are greater probably now than ever before. We live now in a very different world from Cato's. We don't see the large slave gangs of the past. The life of a family house or garden slave is now likely to be more comfortable and more secure than that of a poor free peasant. I should be happy to free Mango tomorrow, but he has begged me not to do it. I shall free him in my will, and leave him enough money to enable him to set up a prosperous business in Priene, together with his wife, one he will be able to hand down to his children. Meanwhile, all the slaves in our family are well fed and cared for, able to marry and acquire money of their own over which I have only nominal control.

Yet even in these days the conditions of life of slaves depends to a great extent on the good will of their masters. Many, including most of the men of my class, would argue that it is better so, and that laws which aim to impose restraint on owners of slaves and owners of land interfere with freedom in an unacceptable way.

There is therefore, at the heart of the matter, a conflict between freedom and justice, exactly as the title of the composition which Hermogenes is planning to inflict on you suggests. This conflict in its turn is at the heart of the political struggles and the excesses to which they give rise that I wrote of in my last letter to you. The resolution of that instability by means of the imposition of an autocracy may be the only escape route known to us, yet it is a hateful one: the love of freedom is natural to us, part of our humanity. Besides, it is obvious that autocracy depends too much on the qualities of one man. For Plato, autocracy, or tyranny as he called it, was the worst of all political systems; for Aristotle, while the tyranny of a bad man was the worst, that of a good man was the best. We have to ask, are there such things as good men in that sense?

Moreover, when it comes to the role of authority in dealing with opposition to its own philosophy, we find that the good Plato recommends methods of repression which could hardly be outdone by the most bestial despot. In his 'Laws' Plato's prescription for "heretics, atheists and Epicureans", whom he does not consider the worst offenders against the truth, is a sentence of at least five years in a House of Correction, where the culprit will see no one but the members of the Nocturnal Council; these are to visit him from time to time and reason with him on the error of his ways. The penalty for a second conviction is to be death. As for the more serious malefactors, such as the founders of immoral cults, they are to undergo penal servitude for life in the most desolate region of the country, visited by no citizens whatever and cast out unburied at death. For good measure, all shrines and sacrifices are to be suppressed, apart from those required by civic worship involving established rituals. I remember the passage well, because of the sensation Hermogenes caused by quoting it during a seminar conducted by a New Platonist philosopher whose reputation among our fellow students Hermogenes and I considered in need of a certain adjustment.

Looking at our own situation, we might be tempted to conclude that the ever present threat of barbarian invasion has proved a blessing for the Empire as well as a curse: the demand that, for mere survival, the possession of the purple has had to become the monopoly of military commanders has at the least absolved us from the excesses of the degenerate monsters who afflicted the Empire in its early days.

Yet the fact remains that we are not free, and cannot read of the noble freedoms of Romans as well as Greeks in the past without becoming sharply aware of how much it is that we have lost. If ever the mere familiarity of our status as subjects dulls that awareness, then it is time to read again Sophocles's Antigone, the greatest text of liberty in all our literature. I should like to know that you had Antigone's speech beginning "It was not Zeus, I think, made this decree" off by heart.

The dream of all men who follow the lead of a humane philosophy has to be that some means can one day be found for creating a new kind of balance between freedom and justice, one that does not result merely from a sort of truce between countervailing political forces representing different interests among the citizens, but rather arises naturally from a feeling of unity and fellowship among them, inspiring them to respect the common good more than their own self-interest.

It is this, more perhaps than anything else, which has stimulated my interest in the philosophy of the Christians. Although I am not entirely sure about the true meaning of what I begin to find in these extraordinary Evangels I am reading, or even whether there is one consistent view on this issue which has been clearly proclaimed by their prophet and which all Christians acknowledge, yet there is at least a suggestion that they see all men and women as, in some fundamental sense, children of God. Evidently, if this is the way they define all humanity in a strictly philosophical way, rather than some vaguely comforting expression which is not meant to be taken too seriously, then the implication is radical, and only too clear. Since in every Roman family the children, the free ones, are (as distinct from the slaves) equal, then it would have to follow that, as children of God, all men and women were equal. The basis of everything Aristotle has to say about distributive justice would not therefore apply: it would no longer be true that men were unequal, with an inequality which reflected their different levels of merit or worth; children are not valued by their parents according to merit, but for the mere inalienable fact of being children. What they have from their father and mother they have as of right, not in so far as they have earned it.

It does not of course follow that Christian justice would mean the distribution of identical amounts of the good things of life to everyone. But it does follow that any variation in allocations made should be not according to merit (however assessed) but in response to need. This is indeed what parents - good parents, that is to say - invariably strive to do; they love, honour and value all their children equally, and they express this equality of value by distributing the resources of the family among the children, not in identical amounts and forms, but to each according to his or her need.

Before I got my brother's letter and had to come here, I had the opportunity for a first discussion of this question with my new friend the bishop with ambiguous results, I must confess. In one sense what he had to say could not have been more encouraging. He quoted an important early Christian philosopher named Paul (his writings are included among the holy scriptures of the Christians. I shall have to tackle them one day when I have a good deal of time at my disposal; they do not look all that easy). It appears that Paul, as well as being an energetic propagator of his faith and formidable intellectual was, like your dear grandfather, an incorrigible correspondent; he used to write letters of exposition and exhortation to various Christian communities, one of his most famous epistles being addressed simply "To the Romans", something a great deal more ambitious than anything I have ever attempted. Philip tells me by the way that Paul on one occasion visited Athens and got into dispute with the Stoic and Epicurean professionals there.

In this Roman letter, so the bishop tells me, Paul insists that God is "no respecter of persons", and when I asked him whether this included slaves as well as free men of all races he was quite emphatic that it did; indeed in another of his letters Paul says explicitly that among Christians the terms "Greek", "Jew" and "barbarian", or "slave" and "free", simply do not exist as means for defining what a man is. However, our stichomythia then went something like this:

LUCIUS: Does this mean that, since God respects us all, we are also to respect each other without distinction?

PHILIP: Certainly each other. More than that, we are commanded to love each other.

LUCIUS: So Christians are expected to love everyone, without exception, even those who do not believe in their God, even those who persecute them?

PHILIP: Indeed they are, Lucius.

LUCIUS: God is the Father of all men and all women?

PHILIP: Of course, yes.

LUCIUS: And so God loves all men and women equally, and loves and values them equally because they are his children, even those who do not believe in him, even those who persecute people who do?

PHILIP: No, my dear Lucius, that you cannot expect. God is the father of all in the sense that he is the creator of all, but only those who believe in him have the possibility to become his children and have the full benefit of his love.

I was tempted to remark at this point that it seemed, if the bishop is right, that Christian men and women are expected to be more loving than their God is, even though all love is said by them to originate from him. But I felt there was probably a misunderstanding on my part, and (to be honest) did not want the bishop to think I was merely stupid.

I was disappointed too when we went on to discuss the Christian vision of slaves and slavery. It is certain that slaves as well as free people are welcomed as full members of the Christian Church, and that many thousands of slaves have been attracted to it and found comfort and support in adhering to it. And I am quite prepared to believe that Christian kindness has influenced Constantine and others in their measures to improve the lot of slaves throughout the Empire. But when I asked the bishop if this meant that his Church would work to raise all slaves, at least all those who are believers, to the level of free people, since all men were equal in the sight of God, he told me that I was not to suppose that the ultimate rewards of faith are of this world; it is in the life to come that all believers will be united in equality. This did not, as you would imagine, satisfy me, but I felt that I had pressed the good bishop enough for one day and held my peace.

I must add that the bishop is planning to send one of his ardent young disciples to Priene, to take over the leadership of the small but growing community of Christian believers there.

He will be what is called a deacon. I hope he doesn't make trouble.

I can hardly wait to get home. The lower town here is already dry and dusty, and even on the acropolis the asphodels are already past flowering. I am longing to see the yellow and purple phlomises and the white and pink cistuses of my Mycale; they will be at their grandest now. We settled for twenty three species of orchid by the way.

4. PRIENE, June

First, I must tell you of the storm of human turbulence that greeted me on my return from Pergamum towards the end of last month.

You may remember that I told you of the bishop's intention to appoint a junior priest of his religion, what they call a deacon, to live and work here in Priene. This happened while I was away, and a young man called Mark duly arrived, to be taken into the home of my fellow councillor Melisandros. Now Melisandros is a native Carian by descent, but nonetheless respected in the local community for that. He is the leading Christian in the town, and the Christians hold their acts of worship in the privacy and safety of his house.

Melisandros is a tactful and discreet person. During the persecution he did not hesitate to perform the necessary act of worship to the emperor, and - very sensibly, in my opinion - advised his fellow Christians to do the same. The young deacon Mark, however, is a man of very different character. He is evidently given to extreme opinions and excesses in the presentation of these, a zealot with a great deal more courage than good sense and no more discretion than a buffalo.

In spite of this, the peace of the town was not seriously disturbed by his public harangues for the first few days, so that Melisandros was, he tells me, beginning to feel confident of the future, when the energetic Mark launched into a public attack on the worship of Athene the Guardian of the City, actually calling for her temple to be destroyed and a Christian basilica built in its place.

Now you know all about my scepticism as to the very existence, let alone relevance, of the ancient and traditional gods. But you know too, I believe, that this is balanced by a certain respect for custom, fortified by a love of all that is beautiful in the old ceremonies and festivals, and a compassion for the love and fear which the common people feel for the patron god or goddess of their city. There is something touching in their faith that he or she is always with them, never deserting them even in the times of greatest hardship or disaster.

Inevitably, Mark's words caused great offence and quickly incited a disturbance among the kind of people who always seem to be on the scene when trouble is afoot. Melisandros, who was luckily nearby in the Council House at that moment, ran to the scene just in time to release Mark who was on the point of being arrested by the men of the watch.

For a few days, it seems, Melisandros was able to keep Mark under some kind of control. On the very evening of my return however one of his men rode into the yard of our villa in a state close to panic, with a message from his master saying that the Christians had stirred up a full scale riot in the town and begging me to bring what help I could.

Mango quickly got together some of the men and armed with staves we set off two to a horse for the town. By the time we got there, Mark and the little group of followers huddled round him were in danger of their lives. There were no signs of the watch, who had simply fled the scene. The mob had the Christians cornered by the main steps to Athene's temple, and were happily occupied in pelting them with stones. Already one of them had fallen, and all had received an injury of some kind. Mango and my men forced our way through the crowd easily enough and once we had got Mark on to my horse Melisandros managed to persuade the leaders of the riot to leave the other Christians alone.

When I got Mark home I handed him over to the women who made a great fuss of him and dressed his bruises, none of them serious. We then gave him a good meal and made him drink some wine, something which he seemed absurdly reluctant to do. The girls had obviously taken an immediate kindness for him; he is young, strong and good-looking and it is true that one cannot help being charmed by his innocence. However I asked him, rudely enough, if he wanted to make a martyr of himself, and was deservedly paid out for my lack of politeness when he replied that that was what he yearned for above all things. No doubt that explains why it did not occur to him to thank me for having rescued him from a particularly nasty death.

Next day I took him off to Miletos to see the bishop, who, I must say, treated the whole affair with commendable calm and wisdom. He told Mark firmly enough that if he did not throw his life away he had every chance of living to see all the old temples in the Empire closed if not thrown down. What all Christians had to do was to trust the Emperor, and leave it to him to give the orders which would ensure this. Meanwhile, the task for Mark was to make himself and his immediate disciples respected and liked in the community by behaving in a way that would make them popular and preaching the good news from the Holy Book. This was all such obviously sound advice that there was nothing for Mark to do but accept it. Besides, to his credit, he was in a hurry to get back to Priene to bring comfort to his unfortunate friends, and was I daresay ready to agree to anything in order to escape from the bishop's admonitions.

I accepted the bishop's invitation to spend that day and the following night with him. I was ready enough to brave a frugal supper and a hard bed in return for the chance to discuss his Bible and his faith at rather more length than we normally could. We spent the afternoon cooling off in the baths, and this gave me the opportunity to ask the bishop about something Mango had discovered in one of the letters of Paul which seemed to be in conflict with what he says elsewhere about men and women being equal in the sight of God. I should explain that Mango, having finished with the Evangels, is now busy transcribing all these letters; the passage which he has drawn my attention to happens to be in a letter written by Paul to what was already an important Christian community here in Ephesus; in it he is insistent on the duty of wives to be subject to their husbands. Mango was delighted at this text, which he bore in triumph to his dear Samia, not a woman known for weakness of personality. This bald notion of subjection not having been well received at the domestic level, Mango referred the matter to me, and I in my turn to the bishop, who proceeded to make what I thought a somewhat over-subtle distinction between equality of value in the eyes of God and equality of status in the systems necessarily instituted by mankind in order to ensure survival and welfare in a more or less hostile world.

Naturally enough, he made the comparison with the inequality which necessarily exists between master and servant and between ruler and ruled in the political system, both matters dealt with by Paul in this passage and others. Feeling as I did in an argumentative mood, I put it that the question of men and women was quite different. In Plato's 'Republic' women were to have equal authority with men in the ruling philosophic class. Moreover, it was clear that in the ruling families at the heroic dawn of our civilisation the status of women was quite different from that which developed after the invasion of Greece by the Dorians; one had only to remember the parts played in the great myths and tragedies by such splendid figures as Clytaemnestra and Antigone, as Ariadne, Electra and Medea, to have the proof of that. In the natural world of animals males are by no means always dominant over females: the she-lynxes on our Mycale are quite as powerful and resourceful as their mates, and everyone knows that Virgil was wrong in supposing that colonies of bees are ruled by a king.

A little less easy for Philip was my suggestion that if there is indeed only one true god, then, when selecting the metaphors we use to describe the divine person, we should allow 'mother' as well as 'father'. Otherwise, in principle, we could find ourselves straying without noticing what we were doing into anthropomorphic folly, the hidden implication being that god is possessed of those organs which distinguish males from females, in the manner of Zeus, Poseidon and the rest; while, in practice, the use of a male metaphor alone could be used as the foundation on which to build an ungodly and unRoman domination of males over females in society. Indeed, I added, the desire to ensure and perpetuate that domination might explain why tradition admitted the dangerously physical notion of the god's fatherhood. All this Philip took in good part, without (not to my surprise) agreeing with any of it.

But the mood changed abruptly when I spoke (disingenuously, I have to admit) about the majestic figures of Hera, Athene and Artemis as the great sculptors and vase painters imagined them. I cannot really blame Philip for getting cross with me and saying that he was shocked at my bringing such a reference to pagan idols into a serious conversation with a Christian prelate. But with my usual perverse tendency to defend the ancient gods from any attacks other than my own I replied that, whatever one thought about the gods, to stress subjection in the relation between men and women may be all right for Greeks and Jews but would never do for Romans. For some reason this made the bishop lose his temper. He told me that it was blasphemy to doubt the words of the Bible, and that I should watch my tongue if I did not want to burn in hell for all eternity. We then both went into a sulk, and did not speak again until later, back in the bishop's unpretentious house, Mango came to tell me that supper, such as it was, was ready.

The bishop's generosity with his wine, which makes up in strength what it lacks in refinement, soon had us friends again, and the bishop, now in good heart once more, launched into a long explanation of the controversy currently raging among Christian thinkers about the true nature of their prophet (if that is what he was), the mysterious Jesus Christ himself. It seems that our bishop, together with a large number of his colleagues led by a leading philosopher in Alexandria, asserts that the Christ was both divine and human at the same time, whereas another learned believer, one Arius by name, holds to the theory that the Christ was simply a human being, albeit a perfect one created by the god for a unique mission. Now it seems that this Arius has an immense following, even among bishops here in Asia, in spite of the fact that he has been officially expelled from the community of Christians for wrong belief - 'excommunicated from the church as a heretic' is the terminology the bishop uses. There is, the bishop says, talk of a plan forming in Constantine's mind to call a Council of all the bishops in the Empire in order to resolve the dispute, something that has of course never happened before. There is already competition to be the chosen location among some of our leading Asian cities - Ancyra, Nicomedia and even Nicaea are mentioned; no doubt there will be fat profits to be made by city traders meeting the many and various needs of such an elevated assembly. The bishop is highly excited about this, and confident too that the Emperor will somehow see the right conclusion is reached and the views of the Arians are finally put to rout.

Partly owing to the effects of the bishop's wine, partly to a certain opacity of the subject matter, I have to confess that I fell asleep at one point during the bishop's rather prolix exposition. It is very likely therefore that I have missed the point, which is something to do with ideas about the nature of the god which are (as I am beginning to understand) in origin Jewish rather than Greek or Roman. For someone of our culture there would seem to be nothing to be said in favour of Arius's version, since it is obviously the less inspiring of the two, whereas the alternative does not seem to raise any serious problems for the philosopher. In much of our greatest literature we are used to encountering heroes who are thought of as both human and divine, or at least 'godlike' to use Homer's favourite word; just as is the case with Codros here in Priene, so in Greek colonies from the Crimea to Spain their human founders are worshipped alongside the Olympian gods; even the philosopher Epicurus is "that godlike man" in the words of our beloved Lucretius; and of course it has been the custom throughout the Empire to worship the Emperor himself as a god.

Fortunately I woke up before the bishop had finished and heard something at least of what he had to say about the Jewish vision of the god as a being not only unique, all powerful and all knowing, the creator of the universe and all that is in it, but so sacred, so holy, that even his name may not be written down. This is something eastern (even the Persians and Babylonians, I am told, never regarded their kings as gods), something very different both from the one almost impersonal supreme being of our philosophers and the many starkly personal gods cultivated by our common people. Little wonder that the Jewish elders could not accept the claim of this Jesus to be not merely the greatest of all the prophets but the son of the god and therefore himself both truly god and truly man. And the other side of that apparent paradox must be that if that claim is after all true then the meaning of the life and teaching of this man-god is not merely more important in degree than those of other philosophers or prophets but quite different from them in kind.

There is, I am afraid, more I need to say about all this, resulting from the first impressions I have from my own reading of the Evangels, but first I cannot put off any more what there is to say about family matters. I was of course greatly delighted to hear that you have seen your uncle Lucius when he arrived among the staff of the Caesar Crispus for the official visit to Athens. There is great joy here at the news both of his good health and of the high regard in which he is held by so great a person as the Emperor's eldest son. We have also hugely enjoyed your lively account of the formal proceedings of welcome accorded to the imperial scion in the Odeon. I can easily imagine Hermogenes's comments on what it means to debauch a language during the laudatory Latin speech given by the fashionable panegyrist the Caesar had brought with him from Trier. Thank you for sending me the text of Hermogenes's own very different Greek address. It is as we should expect in the purest Attic style of Lysias and Isocrates, without any of the Asiatic excesses he and I dislike so severely. I hope he did not incur the Caesar's displeasure by concentrating his praise on the father rather than the son. The effect I found truly impressive, and the comparison of Constantine with Alexander, eloquently and cogently presented as the two greatest reconcilers of east with west, entirely just. He will forgive me for reserving judgment on his treatment of the religious question in this context. I agree of course that an essential part of that union is the reconciliation of oriental and classical religions; Alexander we know understood how the "sharing of customs is a great step towards the softening of men's hearts". Yet I am beginning to doubt whether we can any longer simply group Christianity together with the other eastern cults such as that of Mithras or Isis.

I have kept the most important and exciting news until now. I have had a letter from your father. He is back safely over the Danube in New Dacia, reporting to his provincial governor in Sardica and then to the vicarius of the dioecesis on the outcome of his trade mission among the Gothic chiefs in Old Dacia. He seems to have had some success, and there is a good chance of a revival of the wine and gold trade, with perhaps even the possibility of restoring some of the Roman presence and way of life north of the river. What is more, much more, he is planning to visit us, and hopes to be here next month: I need hardly tell you that the mere possibility of this has put the women of the house into a frenzy of preparation. Naturally it is your mother who is most deeply affected, yet the most interesting phenomenon is not her own emotional state but the quite new status she is accorded by all the other females in the family, not excluding your grandmother.

On every point affecting the welcome due to your father Caelia is deferred to as if she, not Helvedia, were the family-mother; she is permitted to do nothing and required to decide everything.

Nor is this all your dear father says: he has every hope of being able to make the detour across the Aegean to visit you in Athens after his time with us and before he has to return to his province. I tell you all this, although I realise you may have heard it from your father directly already.

After that news, I hope you are in a good enough mood to bear with a little more philosophising. My first reaction to our reading of the Evangels is one of great confusion. I am in a Catullan dilemma, 'odi et amo' , not exactly an 'excruciating' experience but to say the least disconcerting. Almost all the family, after our daily readings under the plane tree, share my bewilderment.

Our problem is that we are impressed - that is too weak a word, 'inspired', even 'transported' would be better ones - by things in these accounts that (I do not exaggerate) we find more lovely and more wonderful than anything I or the rest of us can think of in all our reading or other experience, and yet we are constantly coming across passages which seem at variance with this sublime message if not directly contradictory of it.

The inspiration, to take this first, is of two interrelated kinds, what the Christ said in his teaching on the one hand and what he did and was on the other. The heart of the teaching is absolutely clear and astonishingly simple: the god is a god of love and, for that reason, the whole duty of man is to love the god and to love all other men. What needs attention however is the nature of this love: it is not of course the erotic love of those who are in love with each other's bodies, but it is not either the love we feel towards those whom we have chosen and who have chosen us for the rites of friendship. It is much closer in quality to the love which parents and children and brothers and sisters have for each other. Its essence is therefore to be non-discriminating. It is easy to see how the love which comes from the god is the force behind all creation and the impulse behind all procreation, just as Lucretius imagines the goddess Venus to be in the invocation at the start of his poem. At the same time this love, divine love let us call it, is profoundly humanistic, since when practised among men it annihilates all discrimination due to race or sex or status and has the power to unite all men, Romans, Greeks and barbarians, together in one harmonious 'New Empire', what in these writings is called the "Kingdom of Heaven".

As to the actions and character of this Jesus Christ, what shines out is the way in which he exemplifies a life and a death devoted to this divine love which he preaches. This life as he lived it is presented to us as a perfect one, not merely in the sense of being without fault (which in itself could be something quite sterile) but one exhibiting in every situation divine love in action, that is by giving, by helping, by encouraging, by healing and by forgiving without limit. Notice I say 'a life *and a death* : at the end of the story the nature of the god's love is displayed, literally on high, by the sacrifice of himself in the shape of the god-man who is called the 'son of the god' and whose consent to a wretched death and forgiveness of those who put him to it proclaims the forgiveness of the god for all the wrongs of the world.

All this is so clear and in itself consistent and of such stupendous importance that there can be no doubt of the fact that it and nothing contrary to it is the true message and meaning of the life and death of this god-man, nor any doubt of the authenticity of the record we have of it. Yet there is, scattered in an apparently irregular way within these texts, and at times becoming the dominant element in them, teaching of a quite different kind, which presents the god as an angry figure obsessed with the punishment of people's faults and which relishes the description of such punishment in cruel and barbarous terms.

Let me give you an example of how these different kinds of text contradict each other. In what is self-evidently the true version of the god-man's teaching, we are told that we should love not only those who love us but also our enemies; that this is almost impossibly difficult to do is quite obvious but so is the realisation that divine love could expect no less of itself. Specifically, we are told that we should bless those that curse us or persecute us. Yet in other long passages we find the Christ heaping curse on curse against his enemies, that is the religious authorities of the Jews who were responsible for putting him to death. "Ah", you may say, "but those, if they are enemies of the Christ are the enemies of the god himself, and that is quite another thing than the mere enmities which may exist between men". Not so: this would mean that the god's command that we should love our enemies was not a true reflection of the love which is the very nature of the god; since our love is entirely derived from the love that comes from the god, and is at best a mere shadow of it, it is evidently impossible that it should in any way be, or be expected to be, more extensive than that from which it originates.

If you are sensing here the excitement of the scholar who has scented a prey, you are only too correct. The hunt is on! Even supposing that the bishop is right when he tells me that the texts of the Evangels as well as those of the letters of Paul and the other items in what he calls the New Testament part of his Bible were all established more or less as we have them now by the time of the blessed Emperor Hadrian, that would still give plenty of time for those with opinions they wished to promote or suppress to tamper with whatever written or spoken records of what the Christ did or said may have been current within the first few years after his death. And how could it have been otherwise? What I have identified as the 'true message' is far too revolutionary, far too threatening to all sorts of interests in high places and indeed at all levels of society, to have been allowed to pass without some energetic endeavours to dilute or corrupt it. Mango is as excited by the prospect of the chase as I am myself. Together I believe we may be able to seek the culprits out.

Yet another most welcome letter has just reached us, this time from your youngest uncle Gaius in Armenia. The Persian frontier is now so quiet that he too hopes to be able to leave his post soon in order to spend some time with us. If fortune favours us all, he may be here in time to see your father as well as the rest of us.

We are enjoying the last of the roses, as ever coddled so lovingly by your grandmother. But the heat and dust of summer are beginning to settle on us and burn out the charm of our life here. It is time for our little diversion to the north side of our headland, and it is from there that your next letter will come.

I am glad that your essay on Freedom and Justice earned Hermogenes's praise, something he does not give lightly. I am also pleased that you are forming your own opinions of the architectural glories of Athens. I agree with you that we should not despise Hadrian's Temple of Zeus, for all its overstatement. That we owe reverence to the best Greek work is no reason for decrying everything Roman.

It is also pleasing to hear that Hermogenes's granddaughter (I had forgotten her name is Myrto, I'm afraid) is showing an intelligent interest in your studies and even appears to enjoy discussing questions of literature and philosophy with you. Naturally, I approve of this: I have no choice as a former follower of Epicurus, the first of the philosophers to admit women students to his School. And no doubt she has her father's approval too; he was never an Epicurean, but his general ideas on the education and social role of women are more Roman than Greek. I had underestimated the precocity of young females these days - a mistake for which I, in the family circumstances in which I find myself, have of all men no excuse.

5. MYCALE, July

I cannot do anything but start this letter by responding to the news in yours, which has been greeted in the family with an emotion to which the words 'feverish excitement' come nowhere near doing justice. This exhilaration is accompanied by a good deal of feminine scorn poured onto my grey hairs: "Only a man could have failed to read between the lines of his letters" is the general burden of complaint. I am assured that those philosophic conversations between Myrto and you were bound, by the operation of natural law, to have led in a certain sentimental direction.

I shall not, my dear boy, insult your good sense with the tedious admonitions which the old are traditionally expected to inflict on the young in these situations. I have no doubt that, were it humanly possible, Myrto would be in possession of all the virtues and graces which you attribute to her. And I shall not deny that the evident lack of years which you both share is compensated by certain favourable factors in the circumstances, or that an alliance between my only grandson and the only grandchild of my former fellow student and oldest friend would afford me particular pleasure.

I am grateful too for your sensitivity in offering me the opportunity to express any reservations I might have about a marriage between a Greek woman and a member of a Roman family with an ancestry such as ours, above all the only son of an eldest son. Let me assure you that, apart from any other considerations, my allegiance to the imperial destiny would put any such hesitation out of the question; on the contrary, I should regard a Greek and Roman alliance as something to be proud of, a fine affirmation of the duality of our civilisation.

That your father, if all goes well, will be coming to see you in Athens within the next two months acquires now a completely new fortunate significance. Since you ask me to do so, I shall certainly mention this matter to him when he joins us here. From what I know of his character, it will be better if he has time to get used to the idea of this development before he meets you.

You do not mention Myrta's grandfather, although you know that with neither of her parents alive he has complete authority for her future. Naturally, the ladies here assure me that, since he belongs to the obtuse sex, Hermogenes will have noticed nothing of the non-Platonic progress of your converse. Personally, I have my doubts of this; I do not see why his natural perspicacity in social matters should be uniquely deficient in this instance. At all events, the one piece of advice I shall give you is to have at least made him aware of your hopes, if not to go so far as to endeavour to win his approval of them, before he and your father come face to face.

Family affairs here will seem pedestrian if compared to yours. Our little annual migration to the north coast of our beloved headland was safely accomplished four days ago and we are now well into the routines of that time of the year which we all look forward to most eagerly.

It has been an easy year for the men: neither the simple shelters we sleep in under the trees nor even the boats have suffered much during the winds and rains of last winter, so that very little has been needed by way of repairs. The mules carried us and our stores through the usual rough tracks and gullies over the hill without any serious falls or other mishaps. The northwest breeze comes up as usual in mid afternoon, just as the heat is beginning to become wearisome even close to the sands of the shoreline. The water is as warm and pure as ever. There are no jellyfish this year; the girls are convinced that the drawers your grandmother insists on wearing in the sea have frightened them off.

Before breakfast Mango takes one of the boats out early to fish and I with any of the females who can be got out of bed have a good long swim out to join him for the return. Before we are dry we can already smell the fish frying for our breakfast. We are all active in the morning, the women hunting for herbs to replenish our medicine cupboard or preparing dinner, Mango and I at my correspondence and other work, the girls hunting off the rocks for sea-urchins, octopus and squids; Aulia and Marcia are becoming accomplished divers now, though not yet able to compete with their sisters. The girls too are helping me to complete my record of all the maritime plants here; with the damp air by the shore they can stay in bloom long after the inland flowers are burnt out for the summer. The great horned poppies and sea pinks are even more brilliant than usual this year.

We have dug a deeper cold pit this time, and moved it further into the shade of the trees and rocks, so that we can keep our wine cooler. We hope to store our food better this way too, and so reduce the number of tedious journeys the men have to make to and from the villa.

All of us have a long swim before dinner, and after it we retire to the deep shade of the sea-pines and holm-oaks for our daily reading before we rest. Mango has for some time been wanting to show off the work he has done copying the letters of Paul, and it has occurred to me that it could be a welcome thing to have a change from reading the Evangels (in which there is a good deal of repetition). So we have made a start with Paul's first letter, the one addressed simply to "The Romans" which I've mentioned to you already, said by our bishop to be the most important of all.

I cannot say this has been a great success. We all found the early part of the letter frankly disappointing. The "Romans" Paul is writing to appear to be predominantly if not entirely Jews, since his first concerns are largely with the question of the traditionally elaborate and ritualistic Jewish law and with persuading them that the Christian message has superseded it. This stress, and even more the terms in which Paul treats it, strike me as distinctly odd, given that (according to the bishop at least) it was the leading disciple Peter who concentrated his work during those early days on those Christians who were Jews while Paul gave his attention to those who were not - all those whom the Jews called "Gentiles" (a somewhat uncomplimentary expression, unless I am mistaken, not unlike our use of the word 'barbarians'). It seems to me curious too that he should talk of the rewards for goodness and the sanctions for wickedness being afforded "to the Jews first and also the Gentiles" as if it were not merely a historical chance that the Evangel came to the Jews first in point of time, but as if they were categorically different from Gentiles for all time in the eyes of the god, and had some kind of permanent precedence. Even more strange, bizarre indeed, is his use of the term "Jews and Greeks" as if that comprised the whole Christian community. It is simply not credible that someone of Paul's evident intellectual capacity should make such a gross blunder in a letter addressed to "The <u>Romans</u>" .

What all this comes to is that I understand much more

clearly now why the bishop was so reluctant to allow even a man of my background and education to have his own copy of this Christian Bible. Much of what is in this letter is only of legitimate interest to students of the early history of the Christian church, when the relationship within it between Jews and non-Jews was understandably a burning question. The danger is not merely that anyone reading this text now might be deterred from any further interest in the Christian message (as I am afraid the older ladies in my family may be beginning to be). There is an even greater danger, it occurs to me, that a reader might get all kinds of false messages from a misunderstanding of what Paul is really trying to say.

For example, as the letter goes on Paul has important and interesting things to say about the nature of 'faith', which appears to be seen by him not so much (or, not only) as a moral quality equivalent to fidelity but also as a unique and essential form of cognition. Now Paul insists that we can only become acceptable to the god by means of our faith, and that our actions are not enough, may not even be relevant to this. Yet Mango and I wonder whether what Paul means here by "actions" is not the whole practical business of loving other people and so on but merely the carrying out of all the rituals prescribed by the Judaic law. If this guess is right, the scope for misreading Paul's meaning will be extensive and the consequences serious indeed.

Once Paul gets past these Judaic preoccupations, however, his letter takes us deeply into the heart of what the Christian faith is about, and it is easy to see why the bishop attributes so much importance to it. There are besides some remarkably elevated passages, and one in particular where the sublime voice of the Jesus Christ can be heard in all its purity: here Paul tells us we are to bless those that persecute us and not curse them, and that we must not repay evil with evil - the exact revolutionary opposite to the retributive vision of justice which dominates the tradition and which (if I am right) it was a chief objective of the life, teaching and death of the Christ to overthrow.

Mango and I are nonetheless left in a state of considerable doubt about what Paul is really saying about his faith and what he really thinks about salvation, or "justification" as he often calls it. The question is, who has been saved by the sacrifice of Christ and who has not? He tells us that everyone was in a state of sin before Christ, and everyone had the "free gift" of life because of Christ; yet in the next sentence, both before and after Christ we find the word "everyone" replaced by "many". I suspect that what he means is that whereas before Christ everyone was "in sin", after Christ everyone has the possibility of salvation but only those ("many" in his estimation) who actually adopt the faith "are saved".

This would of course bring Christianity safely into the company of the other mystery religions: the benefits are only for the initiates. But I had hoped for something more, and have a powerful impression that the real meaning of the words of the Christ in the Evangels is something quite different. And in Paul's own account of this I am not sure there is not an actual contradiction. At one point he clearly tells us that it is because of our faith that we receive the "grace" and so the forgiveness and salvation of the god; but elsewhere in the same letter he explains that the amount of faith we have is decided by the god ("he deals to every man his ration of faith"). Obviously, whether men have faith through grace or grace through faith is an issue about which we need to be clear; I should even go so far as to suggest that it would be a distinguishing characteristic of two totally distinct and irreconcilable religions.

I have not forgotten that your last letter had two surprises concerning Myrto not one. Not that it was altogether a surprise to hear that she is well on the way to becoming baptised as a Christian, since I have heard from a number of sources that, at least in the bigger cities of the Empire, more and more young people are 'turning to Christ' (as the expression is), including now children of well-to-do and educated parents. I only hope this is not going to cause distress to her grandfather; if she is the person you say she is, then I have no doubt she will choose to act in the ways least likely to cause him unease. At the same time, I respect her choice, and have no doubt that Hermogenes will do the same; as philosophers we have been conditioned to respect the beliefs of others, provided they recognise the Sovereign Good.

I wonder if you and Myrto have ever discussed what the Christians actually mean by salvation, and by the expression 'eternal life' that keeps recurring in their scriptures - and its alternative? If we take the restrictive view (something I am most reluctant to do) then we must ask what fate awaits those who do not embrace the faith. And here yet again I seem to find myself confronted with contradiction and confusion. Paul in this same letter says that "the wages of sin is death", and this would imply a simple contrast to the 'eternal life' promised to believers. Yet elsewhere in these scriptures we encounter the notion that non-believers will be condemned to eternal punishment, of an inexpressibly horrible kind. This would accord with the view that the soul is immortal because of its fundamental nature, regardless of its moral condition; but as an opinion, whatever other merits it has would seem to be of a much less enlightened nature.

It is interesting, is it not, that the belief in immortality of the human soul has played a much more central part in the philosophy of us Greeks and Romans than in that of our eastern neighbours? What however we have signally failed to do is to prove its truth. It remains a question of pressing concern not only to old men like myself, who are not far from the realm of death by the laws of nature: owing to the lawlessness of men, there is not one of us who may not have to come to the end of life in this world without warning.

There are of course possibly two issues here, not one; whether there is life after death, and, if so, what that life is like.

In all the Schools of the world, I dare say, study of this problem starts with the three arguments in defence of the soul's immortality attributed in Plato's 'Phaedo' to Socrates's last discourse before his execution. I was delighted to read in your letter before last that you take a sceptical view of the Socratic authenticity of almost everything which Plato puts into the mouth of his master in his Dialogues; it is a question which has provided more or less innocent occupation to generations of Alexandrian scholars, but I believe we can now take it as largely resolved, precisely on the lines you suggested to me.

At all events, we can be sure enough that Socrates himself was not responsible for the 'myth' with which the 'Phaedo' discourse ends, and which describes an afterlife where according to their deserts the dead are allocated to a hell, purgatory or paradise not unlike those of which the Christians are said to speak, combined in a somewhat confusing way with the notion of transmigration taken from the Orphic cult; we can be sure of this because it conflicts with the sublime agnosticism of Socrates's final remarks, at the end of the trial in which he was condemned to death: "Now it is the time to be off, me to die, you to live: but which of us has the happier prospect is unknown to anyone but the god".

Before that in 'Phaedo' we have the main arguments in support of belief in immortality. However much or little they retain of Socrates's own words and opinions is immaterial, since it is clear that they depend for what cogency they have on Plato's central theory of the sole true reality of the Ideal Forms of things, to which the human soul, pertaining of the divine, has affinity. You may not have read yet that in his 'Phaedrus' Plato adds another line of argument which is certainly his own: the soul is something which 'moves itself' and therefore cannot be mortal. I have always found this argument too abstruse to be understood; you will have to consult Hermogenes if you want an explanation of it.

In his 'Laws' on the other hand we find a much more complete and satisfactory account. All motion, all creativity, is the work of souls, and the world itself the work of the 'best soul' which is the god; the world is governed not by chance but by conscious design. No doubt you will have heard much in Athens of the still fashionable views on this topic proclaimed by the disciples of the great Plotinus in the New Academy: Mind has become superior to Soul; the One (that is, the god) is the cause of all existence and all values; man is a microcosm, containing in himself all levels of existence, including Mind, by means of which he may achieve communication with the One and hence Ecstasy even in this life. No doubt Plotinus was influenced by Aristotle as well as the Academic tradition, since Aristotle had already elevated Mind above Soul: the latter, being the vital spirit, is linked to the body and therefore dies with it; the former is independent of the body, is linked to the universal mind and is therefore immortal. What is common to all these approaches to the problem is a deep if somewhat elusive belief that the soul of every man is in some sense divine or at least has an affinity to the divine. This sense of the kinship of man and god is, I feel, very Greek, very Roman, very un-Jewish; I am quite prepared to believe that Socrates felt it to be true without being able to assert it as proved or provable.

As a young man I found all this kind of speculation rather tedious, and I should not be surprised if that is your experience too. My own predilection, as you know, was towards the system of Epicurus, and above all the supreme poem in which Lucretius expounds it; I have never denied that my estimation of the philosophic force of that work may have been influenced by the extent to which I was captivated by its power of expression and linguistic beauty. Be that as it may, the atomic theory always seemed to me far more convincing than any other account of the physical world and our perception of it, and still does. At your age I was entirely content with that part of it which described the soul too as made up of atoms albeit exceptionally fine ones, and therefore subject to dissolution at death. A reservation which however I have acquired later in my life derives from my having had to admit that Lucretius's version of the divine - a number of gods living in a paradise and entirely oblivious of human affairs - is little better than puerile. Either we should have the courage to be atheists (which is what Plato took the atomists to be) or we have to give some meaningful account of the relationship between the human and the divine. That, as an imperial servant and someone who has always taken public responsibility seriously, I have become increasingly dissatisfied with the individualism and quietism to which followers of Epicurus are so devoted, is another equally important point of disillusionment, though hardly relevant here.

Yet when we come to the implications which our views about death have for our daily lives, the importance of the Epicurean tradition becomes again paramount. From the earliest times we know of, ideas about the nature of life after death have been confused and tending towards extreme fantasy. If they could not find a destiny for great heroes, the ancients assigned them absurdly to the stars; yet in Homer even so great a figure as Achilles is condemned for ever to a shadowy existence as a bloodless and joyless phantom; judgment and punishment have a place, yet only the most spectacularly evil men and women, such as Tantalus and Sisyphus, or those daughters of Danaus who murdered their husbands, appear to be the eternal victims of an active torment. Yet by Lucretius's time, alongside Orphic and similar cults which preached the doctrine of transmigration, there was an increasing obsession with this idea of judgement, leading to the possibility of eternal punishment administered by demons in hell.

This is why it is so important to study carefully the difficult but critical passage in the Third Book of Lucretius's poem where he first glorifies Epicurean materialism for its having liberated mankind from the fear of death, which (rightly or not) he identifies with fear of punishment after death, and then takes our breath away by going even further than that, developing one of the most astonishing lines of thought in the whole of ancient literature: that it is the fear of punishment after death which promotes the aggression, the hatred and perhaps all the other forms of active wickedness so characteristic of human behaviour. So far from acting as an effective sanction and helping to control the way men behave to each other, Lucretius believes that the fear of eternal punishment is the cause of a kind of universal morbidity, a pandemic disease we could say, which makes men hate each other, stimulates "greed and the blind lust for power", makes us "welcome a brother's tragic death with heartless glee", impels us to "hate and fear the hospitable board of our own kin", even drives men to suicide. It is as if the fear of eternal punishment being itself irrational entails a universal dethronement of Reason, the realm of human conduct being usurped by Paranoia.

When Longinus gave us this passage to study, Hermogenes and I were the only ones in the group willing to defend it from the charge of being fantastical nonsense; it was this alliance which first cemented our friendship. It is, as you will find, a piece of writing which for all its vividness is not transparently clear or altogether satisfactory; yet as a young man it inspired me and I still believe it contains a uniquely important insight. If the fear of punishment after death is one of the prime causes of human wickedness, if not its predominant cause, then may it not follow that the whole notion of punishment is evil, diabolical rather than divine in origin? This would finally confirm my provisional opinion and growing conviction that for the Jesus Christ who proclaimed the god as the source of love to have taught also the eternal punishment of sinners is a simple impossibility.

Yesterday one of your father's men arrived here with news that his master will be with us tomorrow. Already a great feast is being prepared: we shall roast lamb over a huge fire on the open sands. You will have guessed that we have delayed the festivities for the seventieth anniversary of my birth in order to combine the two celebrations. The women, while still sober, will sing; and then, when sufficiently not sober, the men. Later your father and I shall go apart to where there is no sound but the gentle movement of the sea, and talk the night through.

6. HIERAPOLIS AND APHRODISIAS, August

You will not be surprised to see that I have dictated this while on my regular August visit with your grandmother to Hierapolis. I am afraid it will reach you a little later in the month than usual. I do not trust the courier service from here, and shall wait till our return to the villa so that I can have this taken over to my merchant friends in Samos with your other letters in the usual way.

The heat down in the town here is quite abominable, and the teeming crowds of visitors make it even worse; mercifully our lodgings are a little way up the hill, so that cooler breezes and relative peace in the evenings give us the chance to recover from the exhaustion of the day. Why we come here at this time of year you may well ask. Well: there is little to do on the farm, with the hay and earlier crops all in and the vines and late fruit trees not yet ready, and even less to be done in the way of botanising. But the real reason for coming now is that after our return from our vacation on the north shore there is always a sense of anticlimax, so that a certain depression descends on us all. This, combined with the oppressive humidity which seems to get worse every day from now until the first rains come, means that the quality of family life at this time reaches its lowest level in the year. Frankly, I believe the others are only too glad to be relieved of us for a good part of the month.

I know well enough that even my daughter and your mother, not to say the young girls, are convinced that I put up with the discomfort of this place merely to indulge Helvidia's faith not only in the health-giving properties of the waters here but in all the charlatanism that goes with that. It is true certainly that she shows more fortitude than I do when braving a daily immersion in the disgusting brown slime to which this city owes its fame and fortune. For me the principal merit of the medicinal baths is in diverting most of the crowds away from the cold pools of clear fresh water in which I spend as much of my time as I can contrive.

But the true reason why Helvidia and I come here every year has nothing to do with the waters, which are a mere pretext. The real purpose is something much less material and yet more elemental: we simply want to be alone together, and relive, in a certain fashion, the days when we were lovers with time for each other, virtually our only resource being each other and our only responsibilities being towards each other. Keep this inside information to yourself, please; it would only reinforce the sentimental view of the world favoured by the ladies and girls of the family, and would be bad for them.

We came here only two days after your father left us; by the time you get this letter he will have left you too and be well on his way back to New Dacia. I look forward to the news of his time with you in your next letter without foreboding. We talked several times about your attachment, and, although your letter to him on that tender subject had never reached him, he was satisfied with the fact that you had at least written and with what he read in your letter to me. I believe that all will be well.

You can imagine how your father and I had many good stories to share after his recent mission in Old Dacia. You remember perhaps that I spent nearly a year there during the happily brief military phase of my career, when I was only a couple of years older than you are now, and shortly before the Emperor Aurelian of noble memory reluctantly decided to bring the frontier back to this side of the Danube. The old province which Trajan had so heroically won for us was already of course swarming with Goths, and even before my arrival there many Dacians as well as Roman colonists from all over the Empire had abandoned their farms and villas to find refuge south of the river. Yet, in spite of the discomfort and almost daily alarms, I could not help admiring the spaciousness and beauty of the province, the richness of its plains, the grandeur of its mountains and even more the great rolling plateau beyond them. I have only to bring the picture of all this back into my memory to be saddened by the thought of what a great loss Old Dacia is to our glorious Empire.

The poet Ovid has a lot to answer for. We can forgive much of the bitterness of a sophisticated and urbane courtier unjustly banished for life to an outpost of civilisation. But the impressions he has given that the shore of the Black Sea is barely habitable in winter, and that the Dacians are rude and brutal tribesmen - these are unworthy calumnies. The Dacians, what was left of them, I found to be a peaceable and stable people. They have looked after their forests well enough and their great flocks of sheep even better; and they have cultivated their valleys, some as broad and well watered as ours here in Asia, with commendable assiduity. As for their culture, I could overlook the fact that the men wear trousers. All I could not forgive them was the total absence of vines from their fields, all having been rooted up in days long past on the orders of some fanatically ascetic chieftain. Surely it is of that event that our Lucretius should have written his much quoted line about the evil effects of religion.

Yet, 'even the god Hades has his good side' : since before Trajan's time it has been their need for our wines that has persuaded the Dacians into trading with us the limitless resources of iron, gold and silver in their mountains. You will by now have had your father's own account of the reasonable success of his recent mission to negotiate a revival of this trade with the new Gothic overlords. The chieftains are impressed by the current stability in imperial affairs, and certainly would not relish an incursion on the part of Constantine into what they now regard as their territory. It is amusing, is it not, to hear how they are starting to adopt Roman ways, and have even begun to patronise the waters at Aqua Herculis, which is once more operating as a sort of smaller version of this place. And it is good indeed to hear how much Latin is still spoken, even far into the territory of the old province. Yet Aulus is not confident of the security of any of this, and fears that the frontier will need imperial attention again before long.

I shall now let you into another secret. The one part of this time away from home together which your grandmother and I enjoy more than any other, and both enjoy equally, is a brief excursion for a day or two which we always take to Aphrodisias; part of this letter has been dictated from there. I am sure my good friend the bishop would find this quite shocking - not that he would suspect me of holding closer converse with Aphrodite's temple girls than my years or social standing (not to say my wife) would permit, but rather for the quite blatant paganism in which we indulge ourselves at this time. And I am afraid you will think us childish, and find my unphilosophic inconsistency hard to comprehend.

The truth is that we have no guilt at all about our little ritual of thanksgiving to Aphrodite for the erotic joys that have contributed so much to our affection and friendship throughout the half century of our marriage. We love everything about the temple of the sweet goddess and her sanctuary - the lushness of the buildings and their decoration, the explicitness of the paintings and sculptures, the freedom and gaiety of the worshippers, the younger ones among them quite unable to keep their hands off each other. Even the outrageous pictures in the books on sale at every street corner seem to me harmless provided they are taken light-heartedly; they offer me many occasions for teasing your grandmother. Mango and Samia, for all their discretion, cannot conceal from us the pleasure which they too get from all this.

We do not tell the family about these diversions for feelings of modesty in these matters which are natural to people of any education and sensitivity. We are making an exception for you - I say 'we'; I would not write about this without Helvidia's agreement - because it is inevitable that you and Myrta have been much in our thoughts since we visited Aphrodisias. Indeed as well as thanking the goddess for our happiness we have invoked her blessing on yours. As for the two pairs of plump doves which gave their lives in this cause I say nothing but that I hope they contributed to the fare of the temple girls, who look a lot too skinny to me. However, I am told that is the fashion.

Mango and I have set off on a new trail in the Christian Bible, a book written by Luke, the physician who was author of one of the Evangels. It is called the Acts of the Apostles, and tells the story of the first days of the church after the death of Jesus. Mango, who has been reading on voraciously as usual, tells me that much of the later part of this work consists of quite detailed accounts of the missionary journeys of Paul; interesting enough in a historical way but not often taking us to the heart of the matter. The early pages are on the other hand quite sensational. There is an account of great importance of the inspiration of the first Christians by means of a direct visitation of the god; as a result of this all the fears and doubts that had come over them after the death of the master simply vanished. There is also a touching picture of the happiness and solidarity among that first little community, who gave up all their personal possessions in order to share them in common - a sublime arrangement, but not one that lasted for long, I suspect.

Something Mango and I find of particular interest is the evidence for serious controversy quite early in the story. Paul, who had been one of the leading persecutors of the Christians on behalf of the Jewish authorities until he was 'converted' by a mystical experience, emerges as the champion of the vision of the new cult as something universal, relevant and open to everyone regardless of their race or previous religious allegiance. But there was also an influential group who saw their 'faith' as constituting little more than a new Jewish sect. The leader of this group was actually one of Jesus's own brothers, one of at least three men in the story with the name of James; the Jewish people of that day seem to have been as uncreative in the invention of men's names as the old Carthaginians, though I suppose we in our family, with our three Luciuses and three Auluses, have no right to complain.

I find it interesting how patterns in history tend to repeat themselves. A community of enthusiasts operates at first in an informal and highly idealistic way, but before long, as the group wins new adherents and becomes bigger, some kind of structure has to be established. And what happens then is that decisions have to made to which the whole sect or political party then finds itself committed. But these decisions inevitably represent some kind of compromise between contending factions; at the very least they are imperfect, and some of them may be actually damaging to the cause.

So it was with our good Christians: they called a Council at Jerusalem to resolve their disputes. At first reading it would appear that the view of Paul prevailed; at least the Council decided to waive the requirement that all male 'Gentiles' who became Christians should be compelled to undergo the unnatural and barbaric Jewish practice of circumcision - a decision of critical importance no doubt if Christianity was ever going to advance, as it has, beyond the level of a minor heresy of Judaism. But Paul had to pay a price for his victory: James succeeded in insisting that converts were to be told to abstain from various kinds of meat, including any that had been sacrificed to pagan gods, and from fornication.

Now I suppose you can argue that, just as so many years ago the Pythagoreans did, so all religions need to have ritualistic rules about what you can eat and what you cannot, even though

Mango and I cannot find any evidence in the Evangels that the Christ cared at all about such things, rather the contrary. On the other hand the mention of fornication, the only form of behaviour between human beings picked out for interdiction, was a crude error, and one typical of those who all down the years have confused the love of the gods with ascetic practices. It is of no use to argue that erotic excesses were so widespread in those decadent times that it was essential to single them out for elimination. They were no more prevalent, and never have been, than deceit, treachery, envy, avarice, cruelty, slander - you do not need me to extend the list of human wickednesses. To select fornication as if it were uniquely evil is to encourage the notion that 'immorality' actually means, essentially or typically, erotic licence, a ridiculous error which leads to the propagation of endless follies and the condoning of many abominable atrocities.

Sophocles, as everyone knows, considered it one of the blessings of old age that by then a man had escaped from the demands of erotic lust as from a tyrant; Alexander the Great is quoted by Plutarch as expressing his contempt for physical passion. As for Lucretius, his largely hostile treatment of the subject, though graphic, is so idiosyncratic that even his admirers, such as myself, have to confess that his contribution to it is morally worthless. Against all this we must set the glorification of Aphrodite (Venus for the Latins), and all her ways and wiles, by most of the other poets, as well as by sculptors and painters. On the whole, I am on their side.

I have not brought up my children to believe that erotic love between unmarried people is necessarily wrong, and I do not believe that in their turn my grandchildren have been brought up differently by their parents. I have however always stressed that in these matters good men and women should apply the same principles of honesty, loyalty, kindness and the avoidance of excess that they should do in all their personal dealings. And I have equally made clear my belief that once we have married - something which as Romans we choose to do of our own free will - then we should add fidelity to that list of principles. I am greatly encouraged when I find that what I have always held to be right and true on all this appears to correspond exactly with the teaching of the Christ. And even adultery, which - if, as I think, the texts on this point are to be trusted - he does tell us is always wrong, even that is to be forgiven.

Nothing I have said should be taken, my dear Lucius, as intended to refute the view that the deliberate choice of a celibate life can be something positive and fertile of good, whether the chooser is a man or a woman. Jesus the Christ was himself, it seems, celibate, and so was his great apostle Paul; Peter on the other hand was already married when he first met Jesus. The bishop of Miletos has a wife; Mark the deacon has not - indeed he has a tendency to fulminate against erotic love in the way all these ascetics like to do. I must say I wish he wouldn't: it was, I suppose, this kind of zeal which induced the great Tacitus to bring against the Christians the most cruel and wounding charge which they have ever had to endure, that of being driven by 'hatred of the human race'.

Since I last wrote to you about deacon Mark he has, as far as his turbulent personality permits, obeyed the orders of his bishop, and there have been no more civic disturbances. Melisandros tells me that he can now see three groups developing among the men and women of all classes in the town. First there is a small and slowly growing group of ardent converts who are following the strict rules of life set out by Mark and have abandoned any of the old so-called pagan practices; many in this group are slaves or free paupers. Then there is a quite large but rather rapidly dwindling group who are openly resisting the new religion and flaunting their allegiance to the old gods; the majority here are well-to-do folk or self-styled intellectuals. Between these there is a group which is rapidly increasing in numbers and already comprising nearly half the population; they are attracted by much of what Mark says, are influenced by what they have heard of the Emperor's own attitudes and want therefore to think of themselves as Christians and to be called that; at the same time they have no intention of giving up all their former religious practices, least of all worship of the Emperors or of Athene Guardian of the City.

The day before we came away here I had some business to see to in Miletos and paid a call on my good friend the bishop. With great excitement he told me of his latest project, which is to have a church built and dedicated in our very Priene; no doubt this reflects his pleasure at Mark's obedience and recognition of the progress he is making in bringing people into the Christian 'fold'. The project would not of course be on anything like the scale of the basilica whose walls are already rising in Miletos, and which will before long replace the house-church there, let alone what I hear is going on in Ephesos. Both these great churches are being built on the sites where the previous ones were begun only to be destroyed in Diocletian's day; under Constantine's new policy, money is now coming through the provincial finance officers in support of big projects such as these. For us in Priene, it seems that Melisandros has already been able to offer a suitable site for the building on the western edge of the town centre. I immediately said to the bishop that I should be happy to make whatever contribution would in due time be needed to make sure that the project was completed and at a good standard; Philip was duly grateful, embraced me most cordially and assured me that my generosity would be amply rewarded, probably in this world and certainly in the next. Of course I could comfortably afford to fund the whole project, and of course that would be a mistake. In the present imperial climate, there is little doubt that all the town councillors and a good many of the tradesmen will want to be seen to have participated in the venture. If they do, the project will have the good effect of uniting the town rather than dividing it. So, we can foresee how, unless the Emperor changes his vision of these affairs, Jesus will dethrone Athene here step by step and without bloodshed.

Meanwhile on every one of the few occasions when I have stopped to listen to Mark's harangues in the forum, he has not failed to bring in some graphic reference to the flames of hell which, if he is to be believed, are permanently kindled in readiness for the eternal roasting of the ungodly. It is therefore impossible to forget this aspect of the Christian paradox, even if we wanted to. I need hardly repeat what you already know, that this whole notion is for me totally unacceptable, as it is for all the family, yourself no doubt included. Helvidia is particularly scathing on the subject. She has reminded me of that chorus from Seneca's tragedy 'Troas' (you remember how all her family were brought up almost exclusively on Stoic literature) :

> For hell and the foul fiend that rules
> The everlasting fiery gaols
> Devised by rogues, dreaded by fools,

With his grim grisly dog that keeps the door
And senseless stories, idle tales,
Dreams, whimsies, and no more.

Rejection of these childish fantasies is one of the substantive achievements of civilisation; as reflection and the use of reason develop, so our societies are, like children, growing up, and so able to put aside puerilities, including infantile terrors. Seneca was living in a period of unexampled depravity and irrational violence; yet in his words the true voice of sublime reason can be heard. That the noble progress in mankind's vision of his own destiny should be abandoned for the sake of whatever religious enthusiasm is not to be tolerated.

And now I can see a quite new opportunity to resolve once and for all the great dilemma, I mean the choice between two evils which up till now has confronted philosophy with a kind of ineluctability: either as the Epicureans believe our souls are after all mortal and death is the end of everything for all of us, or we have to face the prospect of a judgment which may condemn any or all of us to everlasting misery. If the true teaching of Jesus is that the god is truly a god of love and forgiveness then both these evils are averted, the ultimate destiny of all men being eternal reconciliation and union with the divine.

But, if the true message of Jesus is that it is the destiny of all men to be 'saved', why is it that the generality of even his own followers seem to have rejected it and preferred to persist in the idea of eternal punishment for those who have incurred the god's displeasure? I should be interested to hear your opinion on this, and Myrto's; perhaps you might even interest Hermogenes in the question. Helvidia and I sat up late last night over our wine discussing it, with Mango taking notes of our conclusions. We believe we have identified as many as six solid reasons.

1. Moralists believe that the fear of punishment after death is necessary in order to constrain people, and especially the uneducated and licentious masses, into morally correct behaviour. (We remember here the view of Lucretius that fear of this kind has the opposite effect).

2. The same fear can be useful to the civic authorities, and above all autocratic rulers; it will help to restrain rebels, and, linked to the notion that the authority of the powers that be is established and approved by the gods, the fear will encourage

submission.

3. If the god does not punish, then the moral basis of all punishment exacted by the civil authority is put in question; this would seem to threaten society with anarchy.

4. The generality of men, being naturally inclined to vindictiveness and typically weak at thinking about the god except in an anthropomorphic way, are simply incapable of comprehending the infinite love of the god or of imagining a forgiveness which knows no limits.

5. The same yearning for vengeance can give rise to a lust for cruel and atrocious punishments, which in their wickedness men try to justify as 'deserved' by the victims - we all know what has gone on in the theatres and amphitheatres of even small towns in our own times; if the god himself is addicted to these obscenities then the rationalisation of this indulgence of lust is made immeasurably easier.

6. At the practical level, we may have to incorporate systems of punishment into our attempts to operate justice in society, because we cannot devise an alternative way of defending the necessary laws. Such punishment is right in so far as it is the necessary lesser of two evils; just as a war may be right for the same reason. But punishment, like war, though it may be right, is never good, always evil. Because of their intellectual laziness, men, including many men who ought to know better, fail to distinguish between what is right and what is good. They therefore wrongly conclude that punishment, which may be right, must when it is right be good. Thus they wrongly reach the position of believing that inflicting punishment, being good, is something which the god does.

There: six arguments for you! Do let me know if you find any or all of them valid, and whether you and Myrto have been able to think of any others.

We are leaving for home tomorrow and expect to find your uncle Gaius already there and waiting for us. It was disappointing that he did not arrive while your father was still with us, as we had hoped. But 'better late than never'.

7. PRIENE, September

I have to tell you that your uncle Gaius has been killed in action on the Persian frontier.

We learned of this from one of his legionaries who arrived here in a state of trepidation and exhaustion a few days ago. He had been sent by Gaius's own man Pyrrhos, who has insisted on staying with Gaius until he can have his body embalmed and then bring it back here to us.

The soldier had to be dragged in front of me in terror by Mango and the others. He was convinced I would kill him.

From the account he has been able to give us, Gaius was riding with a small troop of cavalry a few miles over the border when he and his men fell into an ambush. Your uncle, who was wearing his tribune's cloak, was struck through the heart by an arrow almost at once. Our men took him up and found cover, from which they were soon able to drive their attackers off without any further loss.

We had all supposed that Gaius was in no serious danger. The forty-year peace which Emperor Galerius made with the Sassanid Narses has held well and still has over a decade to run. It seems that there has been an irregular group of rebels against the present king, Shapur the Second, operating near the frontier and occasionally raiding over our side of it. Gaius was merely on a reconnoitering mission when the attack took place. It was almost a needless death, which might so easily not have happened. However, there is no comfort in that.

I have tried the consolations of humanistic philosophy. Longinus made us learn by heart what the Stoic patrician Servius Sulpicius Rufus wrote to Cicero, chiding him for his excessive sorrow over the death of his daughter Tullia. Do you know this passage in it?

"There is an incident which brought me no slight consolation, and I should like to tell you about it, in case it may be able to assuage your sorrow. On my return from Asia, as I was sailing from Aegina towards Megara, I began to survey the regions round about. Behind me was Aegina, before me Megara, on my right the Piraeus, on my left Corinth, towns at one time most flourishing, now lying prostrate and demolished before one's very eyes. I began to think to myself, 'So! We puny mortals resent it, do we, if one of us whose lives are naturally shorter has died in his bed or been slain in battle, when in this one land alone there lie flung down before us the corpses of so many towns? Pray control yourself, Servius, and remember that you were born a human being'. Take my word for it, I was not a little fortified by that reflection. This is a thought which, if you want my advice, you would do well to keep before your mind".

I recited the whole letter to the family. But Servius's consolation, for all its magnanimity, does not even touch on what is racking us; it is not our own loss that concerns us all, but our fears for Gaius's soul. Too late, I bitterly regret now my speculations about immortality and eternal punishment; without them, we could all now have indulged the sorrow of loss without this torment of uncertainty, secure at least in the reassurances of Epicurean rationalism. In theory, I was moving comfortably towards a facile confidence in the reconciliation of all men with the god. The impact of harsh reality has annihilated all that complacency.

It is not Gaius's way of life that makes me fear the anger of this Christian god; for all the interdictions of James, I have enough left of rational scepticism to have no apprehensions on account of the Persian girl Gaius has been loving and living with. Yet it must be more serious that, as well as having fallen into many other Persian ways and customs, we know from his letters that Gaius has been drawn far into the beliefs and practices of the Persian religion. The Zoroastrian vision of an eternal struggle between the powers of good and evil is, as Gaius has often pointed out to us, the only explanation of the existence of evil in the world which appears to fit the reality of everyday life. Yet it cannot be reconciled with even our classical philosophers' perception of the sovereignty of the Good, let alone with the severe monotheism which the Christians have inherited from the Jews. For a Christian, a dualistic theology cannot be anything but unreservedly evil, and, if men are responsible for what they believe, then the believer in an evil system must himself be infected by the evil in it, and be liable to the god's retribution.

That the news of Gaius's death came only a few days ago is hard to believe: the strain of which we here have all been victims makes it seem much longer. Helvidia has imposed an iron discipline not only on all the servants but on all the free women too, including herself. The girls move about the house in silence with tear-stained faces; if ever they are overcome, they are told to withdraw, to weep in secret. So even with your aunt and mother; they are not allowed to mourn except in private. As for Helvidia, when we are alone, she consoles me as best she can, herself wooden-faced; she has seen my tears often, I hers not once. All this has been a relentless plan to protect me from the distress which the grieving of women might cause me. Yet it was soon obvious that we could not continue like that for long.

Now, just as the strain of this imposed control was becoming unbearable and reaching breaking point, Mango has come to me and asked permission to tell me of a piece of knowledge he has which he thinks I should be aware of. Over the past months, while the bishop and I have been having our discussions, Mango has been enjoying conversation with the bishop's man, Skyrios; among other things they have talked about the problem which has so acutely exercised the minds of Mango and myself, that of the true message of the Christ concerning the limits of the god's forgiveness. In this context, Skyrios has told Mango of a Christian, a most holy man named Thomas, who was living in Miletos some years ago, and who was known there as Mad Thomas because of the extreme and heretical views which he held and even dared to preach. Chief among these was the idea that it was the destiny of all men to be reconciled with the god, and that the purpose of the sacrifice of the Christ when he was put on the cross was no less than the 'redemption' of all mankind without distinction.

Suddenly, so Skyrios's story goes, Thomas disappeared from Miletos, and it was put about by the Christian community there that he had fled rather than submit to the ritual sacrifice to the Emperor (this was the time of the last abortive persecutions under Licinius). The truth, however, was quite well known to Skyrios at the time: there was a group among the Christians determined to put Thomas to death in order to suppress what they saw as diabolical heresy. It was the bishop who, having a kind heart and a hatred of violence, warned Thomas of the plot against his life and helped him to escape.

What is more, Skyrios has heard that Thomas when he left Miletos sought refuge in Karpathos, that rather lonely and little visited island between Rhodes and Crete. Now and again, rumour comes of his still being there, and that he has acquired a following of disciples among the rude and ignorant local people.

Since I am desperate, I have not hesitated to act on the story. Besides, even if it turns out to have nothing in it, it offers me a good reason for going away from here for a month or so. This will give the women the freedom to grieve as they must, and the servants too who are also suffering from your grandmother Helvidia's implacable regime. Above all it will enable my wife to let her heart break and begin to mend again.

It was evidently with some relief that your grandmother has agreed to my proposal to go with Mango to Karpathos and seek out this holy man if we can. Tomorrow Mango and I will cross to Samos and look out for one of those trading vessels which work among the islands to the south of here.

Our distress here has been mitigated by the good news of your father's visit to you in Athens, and of the happy outcome of his conversation with Hermogenes about the affection which has grown up between you and the young Myrto. You will forgive me for not writing more about that at this time.

8. KARPATHOS, October

I am dictating this in a little hill town, not much more than a village, in the northern quarter of this extraordinary island. It is called Olympos. This is a misnomer, however: the Olympian gods are not in favour any longer here.

Tomorrow the weekly mule train goes from here to Poseideion, the main town and port on the south east of the island. From there I am assured that your letter will get to Delos on a boat carrying a consignment of the famous honey produced on the west coast here; and from Delos there will be no difficulty about it finding its way to Athens, unless the money I have provided to accompany it reaches the wrong pocket on the way.

You will want to know why we are where we are, and how we got here. The voyage from Samos took us all of fifteen days, in fair weather until we had to make the crossing from Rhodes; this was long and rough, so that both Mango and I had a day and a night of terror and nausea. Earlier on, at Patmos and Leros, where the penal colonies are, we could not go ashore, but we enjoyed pleasant days sight-seeing in Kos and Knidos and at Kameiros on Rhodes. Knidos was especially enjoyable; although the worship of Aphrodite is by any standards overdone there, and there was evidence of trouble coming from the growing Christian community. I took the unique opportunity of going to see Praxiteles's masterpiece, the nude marble statue of the goddess in her principal temple. I was not disappointed. The figure stands alone in an open shrine, so that one can admire her glorious form from all sides. I am ready to accept Lucian's judgment that the expression in the eyes and mouth are unequalled, and Pliny's that the work is equally beautiful from every viewpoint, though whether it is, as he thought, the finest statue in the world I cannot say.

I know almost nothing about this island, except that in his Fourth Georgie Virgil (unlike Homer and everyone else I know of) locates the curious polymorphic sea-god Proteus here. The islanders have a dubious reputation, being generally supposed to have lived by means of piracy and by luring innocent merchant vessels on to their rocks. The more likely truth is that their island was used by pirates for many generations whether the inhabitants liked it or not. This, together with the relative lack of fertile valleys and fresh water, would account for its reduced population and comparative failure to have benefited from the general imperial prosperity.

There was no difficulty in discovering in Poseideion where we had to go to find our Thomas, although we were struck by the very different ways our enquiry was greeted by various people: some folk were shocked or unkindly amused by it, others much more sympathetic, even insisting that his nickname was not Mad Thomas but Good Thomas. My impression that the less friendly reactions were usually those of Christians was confirmed when we reached the next sizeable town on our journey north, Aperoi, where there is a well-organised Christian community, with a deacon and hopes for a church building as at our Priene; there is even talk of the appointment of a bishop for the island and a rivalry with Arkaisia on the west coast about where the seat of the new bishopric will be.

At Aperoi almost no one wanted to give us helpful information and every effort was made to deter us from going any further. However, I managed at considerable cost to suborn a good peasant to act as our guide; without him the next part of our journey would have been impossible, since in the middle of this long and narrow island the slopes of the central mountain come down almost to the sea-cliffs on both coasts. The tracks are often difficult to distinguish, and a wrong turning could have perilous consequences.

This part of our route enabled us to experience the breathtaking beauty of Karpathos, excelling anywhere I have ever encountered in all my travels. As well as the extensive cypress forest which clothes much of the hills, there are good patches of chestnut, beech and poplar in the gullies of the foothills. Often the path is little more than a goat pad, with the rocky crags immediately above and the sea several thousand feet directly below. Our guide told us that in the spring the whole island is decorated with a profusion of wild flowers, and that the women (who, he explained, understand these things) boast that there are more orchids here than on Crete and Rhodes put together. Even in autumn, I was not disappointed: as well as sea squills and dwarf squills, the slopes are carpeted with autumn cyclamens and yellow ground-lilies, and the rocks are brightened with the papery white petals of the last narcissus of the year.

Olympos is a pretty village, its one main narrow street wandering up the shoulder of the hillside. All the slopes round about have been laboriously and meticulously terraced - no wonder so many orchids love the place! Though some of the terraces have been abandoned, many are still intensively cultivated; the hopes raised at the sight of abundant vines and of large flocks on the higher slopes have not been disappointed - the red wine is rough but excellent, and the goats' and sheep's cheeses also delicious.

We were immediately welcomed by the villagers as soon as they knew our purpose, and were brought to the neat cottage at one end of the street where Thomas lives. Here we received another welcome, warm but without exaggeration, evidently as if our arrival was the most natural thing in the world, almost as if we were expected.

Very soon we perceived that Thomas is disabled: he has the crippled hip which sometimes afflicts people from birth. He is a small, slender man with a face which inclines to the simian; the mouth is large, the eyes small and bright. His movements and gestures are noticeably graceful, but in a natural rather than studied way; his elocution of Greek is precise and pleasing to the ear. He listens with close attention and converses with ease. He enjoys jokes. But the most striking thing about him is the general effect of his expression and manner, which reveal a harmonious compound of serenity and animation of a kind I have never before encountered.

After contriving to find out a great deal about us in a remarkably short time, including the context and purpose of our visit, Thomas entrusted us to one of the village ladies, having made it clear that we could stay as long as we liked, as his guests and guests of the village - each of these seemed to imply the other. Our hostess is a widow. She has simply taken us into her house as if we were her own kin. She makes no distinction between master and servant; Mango was at first uncomfortable to be eating at table with me and sleeping in a similar bed in the same room, but has grown used to it. I can honestly say that in this place it seems to me the most natural thing I could imagine.

We have been here now fifteen days, and have become quite a part of village life. The people understand the relationship between Mango and me, but are not interested in it.

The last few slaves here were liberated a generation ago; this was not the result of any egalitarian fervour, simply a gradual but inevitable economic development - there was no significant part left for slaves to play in the scheme of things.

Some twenty years ago, shortly before Thomas arrived here, the village experienced a crisis in its history. All the land surrounding it was at that time owned by former villagers who had gone to enjoy the fruits of urban life in Rhodes. But one day, when their agents came to collect the rents, they were met by all the men and boys of the village armed with staves, and given the choice of going away or being thrown into the sea. After this had happened several times, the landowners simply gave up.

There was then a period of bitter dispute about the division of the land, with some families presenting ancient claims and so on. There was violence, and the beginnings of feud. At this point Thomas appeared, soon to be recognised as a holy man, who the villagers believed, as they still do, had been sent to them directly by God. He was invited to adjudicate the whole problem of the land; as a result, about half of it all is owned privately in not very large allotments. Every householder has the right to own some property, even if in some cases it is only quite a small patch; there must be no possibility of a revival of the class distinction between those who are landowners and those who are not. The rest is common land which villagers farm in equal lots for their own use and profit, owing one tenth of their produce to the village elders; the funds thus acquired are spent on projects for the benefit of all or relief of hardship. The outcome is that people can own property and buy and sell it and other goods, but no one is prominently rich and no one uncomfortably poor. Thomas regards this as a compromise, and besides merely a temporary, pragmatic arrangement; he insists on two propositions, the first being that we cannot reach perfect or permanent solutions to these sorts of human problems, and the second that some solutions made for the time being are very much better than others.

The sense of unity in the village and of equality among the villagers is reinforced and indeed guaranteed by adhesion for some years now of all the families to the Christian faith, and acceptance of Thomas as their pastor and prophet. Thomas insists on the doctrine that all human beings are the children of

God, and that this relationship, as is naturally the case with the relationship of parent and child, is inalienable. We as Romans have long been accustomed to the practice of adoption, even in the most aristoctaic families, and to the idea that an adopted son may turn out better than a natural one; and you may remember where Plutarch tells us how Alexander the Great believed that while "God is the father of all mankind, it is the noblest and best whom he makes specially his own". Yet Thomas rejects the notion of Christians becoming children of God by adoption, as a result of their acceptance of the faith. He regards this as a fundamental error, even though it is what the great Paul himself believed and taught.

One of the stories which Jesus told by way of allegory is about a son who claims his inheritance from his father, wastes it all in riotous living, and not until on the point of starvation returns home in shame to beg forgiveness; the father comes out to greet him with joy. This is a 'parable' (as it is called in the Christian scripture) of the relation between man and God, and the orthodox Christians use it to stress that forgiveness is always there however great the fault, yet depends on repentance. Thomas points out that although at his lowest point the young man (as the story has it) "felt no longer worthy to be called a son" he never as a fact ceased at any time to be a son, because that is impossible, whether by choice or by loss of right through misdemeanour. For Thomas the concept of becoming a child of God by adoption because we accept faith in Jesus Christ is a sophism. He deduces from this that any 'fall from grace' however extreme can only be temporary; the destiny of an immortal soul cannot be understood except as that of something 'made in God's image' (itself 'divine' as the Platonists would say).

All this came to light in one of our earliest conversations with Thomas, the length and frequency of which is only limited by our reluctance to enjoy a monopoly of his time. Very soon after that I was able to ask him for the whole truth concerning the salvation and redemption of mankind, the concept of judgment and the visions of heaven and hell. The most important thing I have to say to you in this letter, Lucius, is that Thomas has confirmed for me everything which I was beginning and striving to believe about the truth of Christ's message before my confidence was shattered by the death of your uncle, my youngest son.

With Thomas's encouragement, I set out all the six arguments which I wrote to you two months ago to explain how the notion of eternal punishment, if it were false, might yet have become what is the official doctrine of the Christian Church. Thomas's response was to say that they were all correct. He explained too why the theory of Lucretius that the fear of punishment after death is a cause, if not the chief cause, of human wickedness is so suggestive without being completely convincing. The effect is not as direct, Thomas maintains, as Lucretius supposes; what happens is that the belief in the gods as addicted to punishment becomes a permanent justification for the dominant practice of punishment in human society. This in turn ensures that fear plays a leading part in all human behaviour; indeed, much to the advantage of tyrants, whether in the family, the city or at the level of kingdoms and empires, fear comes to be regarded not only as a necessary evil but as if it were in itself intrinsically good, a natural and beneficial component of relations between men. The reality is that fear is an unmitigated evil; its operation in human affairs is like that of some insidious disease, and the wickednesses of greed and hatred which Lucretius correctly describes are symptoms of that disease. In this way the lust to punish operates both as a consequence and as a cause of the evil in the world. The last word on this subject has been said in one of his Letters by John called 'the Apostle': "There is no fear in love; rather, perfect love casts out fear, because fear expects punishment, and he who is afraid is not perfected in love".

These words of John the Apostle, who is the same as the Evangelist, are of special value to our Thomas because they are part of the tradition in which he places himself in the story of Christian philosophy. It seems that John came to our part of Asia at the time of the dispersal of the Christians from Jerusalem. During the earlier persecutions he was banished to the penal colony on the island of Patmos where he wrote the original form of his Evangel and Letters. On his death, the Christians were allowed to bring his body to Ephesos, where they have now erected a shrine which they keep holy in his memory. His disciples then split into two groups, one of which, the one which Thomas follows, survived only with difficulty among a very few, disregarded devotees. It seems that the revered saint Polycarp, who had known John personally, and who in his old age was 'martyred' by burning in Smyrna, was in this tradition. The other, larger group became much preoccupied with prophetic extravagances, in form and spirit quite unlike anything their master had concerned himself with. There is in the Christian scriptures a book entitled 'The Apocalypse' written by one of this group and purporting to be by John himself. It is, as such effusions commonly are, a mixture of fantasy, some of it dangerous, with passages of high inspiration and great beauty; judging by its author's rabidly hostile attitude to the Empire, it was written during one of the persecutions. Many Christians, including scholars, accepted that John was indeed the author of these exuberances, until as recently as the time of our gallant Emperor Gallienus a bishop of Alexandria proved the impossibility of this.

At the end of this discussion, Thomas reminded us that, if we were truly to understand how difficult it was for the early Christians to receive the full gospel of forgiveness, we should always keep in mind the atrocious persecutions to which they were subjected. We had to remember too that, whereas in our day Jews and Christians have little contact and the Jewish teachers are even dropping the use of the Greek version of their scriptures, in the fifty years or so after the death of the Christ the relation between the two religions was close and intricate, so that the disillusioning effect on the Christians of the Roman destruction of Jerusalem, less than forty years after the death of Jesus, must have been devastating.

A few days later, Thomas began to instruct us on the ways in which the true message of the Christ has been contaminated and obscured by other incompatible ideas interpolated into the original accounts of his life and teaching, whether (as we cannot now know for certain) the pure versions were all or any of them ever written down or whether some or all of them only ever existed in oral form.

I explained to Thomas that our good bishop Philip regarded everything that was written in the Bible as holy, and was deeply offended at the least suggestion that any of it could be even trivially inaccurate, let alone critically opposed to the truth. Thomas, who as we know was a colleague of Philip's in times past, replied that this position was understandable but incorrect. The Bible is indeed not only holy but the most holy of all books in the world, because it contains perfect information and perfect teaching about the most important of all truths. It is however an error to believe that that which contains perfection must be entirely perfect. Such a belief disregards the reality of the human condition; even divine inspiration is a relative, not an absolute, state, while since we are subject to time even a perfect thing may be made imperfect by the later intrusion of inferior material.

In the view of Thomas, it is not possible to read the Evangels in a spirit of rational faith without concluding that there are in them four kinds of text, those sections that are clearly true, those that are clearly untrue, those whose truth is a matter of doubt and those for which there can be misunderstanding about the kind of truth they contain. That there is, and always will be, the third of these categories, is itself another inescapable manifestation of the human condition; there may even, over time, be uncertainties and changes of perception about the first and second. The fourth category consists especially of legends and allegories, which help us to understand important truths but which are not intended to be records of fact; these can be wonderfully illuminating, but at considerable risk, since if readers wrongly suppose they are factual all sorts of follies, errors and disputes can ensue.

I asked whether teaching attributed directly to the Christ, provided it was perfectly true to the content and spirit of his message to the world, would count as in the first category even though it was not expressed, and could not have been expressed, in the exact words spoken by him on one particular occasion, and Thomas replied "Yes, it would". "A little like the speeches in Thucydides's history?" "A little like that, but much closer to the original, much more often using the original words delivered on one occasion or another".

I would not have written about these questions at such length if I did not expect that your affection for Myrto and her attraction to the Christian faith mean that you may have, and wish to share with her, a far greater interest in the problem of tracking down the true character of this faith than you had when you set out for Athens as an open-minded student of rhetoric and philosophy some eight months ago.

Thomas finished his discourse by warning us that there were several forces at work causing alien material to have infiltrated into the Evangels. Followers of Jesus's cousin, called John the Baptist, and of His brother James, though themselves holding quite different opinions, shared a common determination to defend the tradition from the radically subversive teaching of the Christ. Lurid prophecies about the doom of Jerusalem and the sudden calamity which would fall with terrible suddenness on individual people must be understood in the light of the utter destruction of the Jewish city and state inflicted by Titus in the second year as Emperor of his father Vespasian; such 'predictions', even if made before rather than after the event, are extremely unlikely to have been of interest to the Christ whose message was a universal one. Again, a number of passages in the scripture reflect the wrong belief of perhaps all the first Christians that Christ was to come again in glory in their lifetime. They simply could not comprehend that God would not revenge himself on his enemies as they were brought up to believe he always had, and they misunderstood what Jesus meant when he spoke of the coming to them of the Holy Spirit after he had finally left them. Another consequence of the human condition which we have to acknowledge is that a perfect message may be imperfectly understood, even by those for whom it was designed.

The effect on both Mango and me of all that Thomas said has not been a simple one. We are of course enormously encouraged to know that our confidence in the limitless nature of the love and forgiveness of God is not vain. Yet so much time devoted to the awareness of false teaching in the very holiest of Christian books has inevitably left us with our faith in a vulnerable condition. We know much more about what has to be discarded, but are we sure what is left?

Thomas has foreseen this predicament, and prescribed what we must now do to meet it. His remedy is that we are to go apart on our own - I mean not even us two meeting or talking to each other - for three full days. During that time we are to read only the accounts at the end of all four Evangels of the last days of the Christ from the time he had his last meal with his disciples to his very last appearance to them, and to spend all our time reflecting on these . Then we shall meet again with Thomas, and talk about the faith.

I must give Mango time to copy this letter before the mule train leaves tomorrow. It comes with my fondest wishes to you, to Hermogenes, and to Myrto. Mango asks to be remembered to Thrax.

You will have noticed that I am beginning to write 'God' as a name rather than using the expression 'the god' to designate the function. So I am following the Christian way, in variable defiance of both the Greek and Jewish traditions. You and Myrto will draw your own conclusions from this.

9. KARPATHOS AND KNIDOS, November

I am writing again without having heard from you - but indeed I hardly expected that. To state it in bald terms, our mission here is completed and we shall leave to start the journey home the day after tomorrow. Although, to be surer that it will reach you, I shall not despatch this letter until we are back in Samas. I am dictating it now both because there may be no chance on the voyage home, and because I want to set down the events of the last few days while they are still fresh in our minds.

As you might expect, Thomas's prescription of three days of solitude devoted solely to the accounts of the stupendous events before and after the execution of the Christ had a profound effect both on my intellectual grasp of the Christian reality and on my feelings about it.

When Mango and I met on the fourth morning we found Thomas busy with the personal problems of villagers and it was not until after our midday dinner that he invited us to go walking with him. He took us up through the terraces, then by a sheep path round the side of the mountain and finally by way of a narrow pass between two peaks. Though he walked with a stick his progress was surprisingly vigorous and agile, and we had to go hard to keep up with him. As we came through to the western side of the island we could feel the warmth of the autumn afternoon sun. Thomas found a sheltered place, a level grazed area below rocks, and here we sat looking out at the great expanse of the western sea.

We rested in silence for a time. Then Thomas asked with great gentleness what our thoughts and feelings were about all we had read and reflected on. I said that I felt as if the whole direction of my mind had been changed; as if all the hopes I had invested in philosophy since my young days were in the process of being fulfilled and all the doubts I had encountered down the years resolved. I felt like a traveller who after much searching and many false starts had finally found the right path and so was for the first time confident of his arrival at the longed for destination.

Thomas next asked Mango whether he thought the stories we had read were simply true, and he replied, "Yes", he did. And what, asked Thomas then, about the inconsistencies between the various accounts and variations in detail, the omissions of important specifics in one version or another? Mango said that it was like the times when he had been asked to interrogate his fellow servants about some mishap or missing or broken article, for example. Even if everyone was telling the truth as they had experienced it or as they remembered it, yet there were always differences between their various accounts of the same event; the four accounts of the Evangelists seemed to him just like that; they showed exactly the combination of a common core with quite numerous variations of detail that happen when a number of ordinary people are trying to tell the same truth. This reminded me of my experience as a magistrate examining witnesses when I was vicarius of the Seven Provinces, and I agreed.

Thomas then became very earnest in his questioning of us. How could we be sure that differences between accounts did not betray important falsifications? How for that matter could we know that all the accounts were not substantially flawed, even radically false? After all, we had here a story which included someone rising from the dead and reappearing after death, evidently in defiance of the laws of nature. Was this not obviously yet another tedious example of a well-known form of sensational literature concocted by mendacious wonder-workers?

I responded with the usual set of tests that we apply to a text if we wish to put its veracity on trial, and which I am sure that no one who has been a student of Hermogenes for nine months needs to hear repeated. I said that all that we had read seemed to me to pass those tests. But then I tried to express something much harder, which is the feeling we may have when contemplating a text as a whole, a total conviction, more powerful than the sum of any specific conclusions we have come to about it, of its fundamental truth or falsity. We may compare this, I said, to the judgement we may pass on a fellow human being, the certitude that one man may be trusted and another man not.

So it is for me with the accounts of the suffering, death and resurrection of the Christ: the whole shines with a light of truth which cannot be denied. Even so, there are some passages where the clarity of the vision of irrefutable truth glows even more brightly than it does in the rest; the whole account of the last meal which the Lord Jesus had with his disciples, his demeanour when brought for trial before the Roman procurator and the Jewish priests, the mysterious beauty, so tellingly free from all exaggeration or sensational treatment, of the appearances after his rising from the dead. Especially, there is the time just after his rising when he meets one of the women who were among his followers in the garden where he had been buried; the time when one of his friends, Thomas the Apostle, doubts whether the person before him is really the Christ; the time when the risen Christ meets two of his followers who are walking to a village near Jerusalem, and they do not recognise him until he breaks the bread for them at supper; the time when the disciples - do you know, Lucius, that a number of them were fishermen? - bring their boat into the shore of a lake early in the morning to find their risen Master standing on the shore waiting for them. I cannot describe the power of the effect that these accounts have on me; their truth is unquestionably improbable, but their untruth impossible.

Had I found, asked Thomas then, that not one incident in the story belonged to his second or third categories, was simply or untrue or uncertain? "What do you think, Mango?" I asked. "None", said he, and I agreed. "Is then everything in all the four Evangels, from the time of that last supper, to be assigned to my first category, that of direct truth?" I had expected the question, and wished I could simply assent to it. But I could not. "Very nearly", I found myself forced to reply, "but there are one or two details about the crucifixion itself which we have, however reluctantly, to assign to the fourth category, that of legend. The incidents of the natural phenomena and rending of the curtain of the temple at the time of the Lord's death are sensational, and therefore quite unlike anything else in the whole account. I am afraid they are legends that have found their way into the true account of what happened. And there is a practical problem about the conversation on the cross with the two malefactors, which comes only in one of the versions." ("It was in Luke's," says Mango, who remembers every detail much better than I do).

"No doubt what Jesus cried out from the cross could have been heard, but the likelihood of an exchange of words with those beside him being audible to those below is not very great. I suspect this is a legend which grew up among those who wanted to stress the importance of the difference between believers and non-believers in the eyes of God".

Thomas did not say what his own thoughts about this were, but I had the impression that he did not disagree with me. He then asked us if we wanted to become Christians there and then, even though we realised that if it were known that we did not believe in the eternal punishment of unredeemed sinners and non-believers we should be considered heretics. Now that the Emperor was not merely tolerating the Christian religion but actively promoting it throughout the Empire, the position of a Christian heretic might become even more perilous than that of a pagan; the possibility of Christians persecuting one another should not be excluded.

I asked whether there was any hope that our view of the unlimited love of God might prevail, since the self-contradiction involved in the vision of a God who was both all-loving and vindictive was so patent that it must surely be doomed to defeat itself. Thomas replied that we had to trust that one day the truth would conquer the minds of all men; this hope is an essential element in our recognition that we must never abandon responsibility to strive for perfection in this world. However, for the reasons which I had myself analysed, the forces against it were extremely powerful. After the death of the tyrant Caracalla, when the great Christian philosopher Origen was at the height of his influence in Alexandria, there was hope that the truth as we perceive it would become generally recognised in the Church, the intellectual centre of which has generally been in that city.

At this point Thomas asked me whether I had read any of Origen's writings. I replied that when I was a student under Longinus in Athens he was one of the names which we heard mentioned by the professors, many of whom were well read in the works of the Christian philosophers as well as in the Greek versions of the Jewish scriptures. We as students were not however encouraged to concern ourselves with any of this; the New Platonists were then all the fashion, and were making it their business to lead intellectual opinion away from all taint of Christian beliefs. This had set the pattern of my personal studies throughout my life; I had only recently begun to read any but the non-Christian writers.

Thomas then explained that at least from the time of Clement, one of the early 'fathers' of Christian thought in Alexandria, pagan philosophy was studied seriously as a useful preliminary training for those in search of spiritual knowledge. Origen was a scholar in this tradition. He believed truly in human freedom, and refuted the Stoic view of fate: fate may play its part in the consequences of our action but does not determine them. The role of providence is to ensure that in the end all things work together towards an ultimate harmony and reconciliation. Origen however fell from the favour of the bishop of Alexandria, and later was tortured to death during the vicious persecution launched by the Emperor Decius. No doubt evil begat evil: that persecution and the one more recently for which the great Diocletian was so tragically responsible can only have tended to reinforce among Christians the orthodox view that God would be revenged of his enemies; since then little has been heard of Origen or of his theory of reconciliation. All that can be said is that Origen's fine library has survived in Caesarea, and is still being used by Eusebius, the great bishop there who is one of Constantine's chief religious advisers.

I said that all this set a dilemma before us: if Christianity was a religion for all men, it should be practised in a spirit of common fellowship, all Christians being members of one united Church. If then what we believed to be an essential part of our faith, indeed something at the heart of it, was according to the majority of Christians and the highest authorities of the Church a heresy, how could we conduct ourselves? Thomas agreed that it was not possible to be a practising Christian except within the Church, the society of all Christians. What we should have to do would be to conform in all public and shared worship, and keep our deepest beliefs to ourselves, to be shared only with kin and servants. In this way we could establish and maintain pockets or cells where the true faith was understood and practised and knowledge of it preserved for the day when it would be universally recognised and accepted. As a priest himself, he could only do this in a place of retreat such as Olympos, though even there his future would be in doubt once a bishop was appointed in the island. But I could continue to take as full a part as I liked in public life, since the secret truth entrusted to me need be known only within my family.

With this reassurance, first, and then Mango declared our wish to become Christians. As the dusk of the short day began to gather round us, we three then walked back to the village slowly and in silence, full of our own thoughts.

The very next day we were baptised. Thomas, Mango and I with two of the village elders went by mule the few miles down the good track to the little bay on the east coast. Here there is no village, just a few shacks and boat-sheds for the handful of fishermen who keep Olympos in fish and shellfish and very occasionally create a local sensation by the discovery of a pearl. There is a sandy beach, on which we left our clothes. We had to wade out some little way, as the sea is shallow there all along the bay. This was frankly uncomfortable, the water being naturally cold by this time of year, and there was a sharp little wind to take the warmth out of the morning sun. When we reached where the water was up to our waist, Thomas made us go right under it, heads and all. He then made the sign of the cross on our foreheads and said the prayers of forgiveness and acceptance into the Holy Church, and the elders said "Amen". I cannot speak for Mango, but as for myself I was glad to get back to the beach and set about getting myself dry as best I could. Discomfort prevented any warm emotion I might have felt, but I knew that now the sign of the cross had been made on me there was no way back from the commitment I had made and that I was a Christian for the rest of my life, whatever of good or ill that might bring.

Only two days after that it was the Lord's Day - no doubt, Lucius, you have learned the meaning of all these expressions from Myrto by now. We went with all the village up the hill to a place where there is a natural concavity in the shape of a small theatre; in the centre of the level space at the bottom, the villagers have built a rough altar out of rocks and stones from the mountain. We sat on the grass of the slope, about two hundred of us, including the children and infants in arms. Thomas came then, together with a number of boys and girls of the village, all about fourteen or fifteen years old, there to help him. The girls carried baskets of bread and the boys had big amphorae of wine, carried by the handles, one between two of them. Thomas was carrying a silver cup and a silver plate with a fish on it, which he put on the altar. The bread and wine were for us to consume at the Eucharist, but the fish was there only as a symbol of the

Christ, the Ichthys, and reminder of the fishermen who followed him and how he waited for them at the shore of the lake after he had risen.

Thomas talked to us about the true faith. He read to us the story in the Gospel of John about the woman who was guilty of adultery, who was about to be stoned to death until Jesus stopped the execution with the challenge that the man without sin should throw the first stone. Thomas told us that it was especially important that Jesus then told the woman that He did not condemn her, although there was nothing said about her having repented.

Thomas warned us that this story was too difficult for many Christians to understand, including some of the most important among the leaders of the Church. The reason was that most people, even committed Christians, were not able to reach up to the comprehension that the loving forgiveness of God knows no limits - it was too much above anything they had ever imagined to be possible, and too much for the victims of horrendous persecution to take to their hearts. They preferred to hold on to what they could understand, the old, old belief that an adulteress deserved to be punished, and that God would want her to be punished because he was himself a punishing God. And the people who suppressed this story were of course men, who had their own reasons for wanting to believe that the last thing in the world that should be forgiven by God or man is the adultery of a wife.

But the story ends, Thomas went on, with Jesus telling the woman to, "Sin no more". Raising his voice, Thomas then asked us all whether we thought the woman committed adultery ever again. And some of the young men of the village and men in the prime of life, only these, cried out at once "No, Good Thomas! No!". "You are right", said Thomas. "It is not that we are forgiven because we do not sin, but that we are helped not to sin because we are forgiven. Men try to eliminate sin by killing the sinner; their price for freedom from sin is death. God offers us both freedom from sin and life".

Thomas then went on to remind us of many other passages in the Evangel where the true Christ reveals himself to us. We must forgive our brother who sins against us not seven times but seventy times seven; we must not judge others, or we may be judged ourselves; that we should love one another is not something which has always been acknowledged, it is the new commandment. In the special prayer which he told his disciples to use, and which the Christians call the Lord's Prayer, we are to pledge that we shall forgive those who sin against us, and this is the only obligation linked to the forgiveness which God affords to us, and the only one mentioned throughout the prayer. Christ the Good Shepherd tells us he has other flocks which 'are not of this fold' and promises that in his Father's house 'there are many mansions'. And on the cross the Christ prays to God to forgive his executioners who did not know what they were doing. Stephen, the first martyr, did the same, praying as he died that the sin of his cruel execution by stoning should not be charged against its perpetrators. Above all, Jesus laid down his own life as an atonement not for the sins of members of any Church or sect but for those of mankind; as John the Apostle says in his Letter, the Christ has propitiated not for our sins only, the sins of Christians, but for those of the whole world.

We must not suppose that our reward as believers is something that we shall have for ever in an after life which non-believers will not have; that is not true, and as a presentation of the way the justice of God operates is both absurd and blasphemous. The reward that believers enjoy is immediate, the knowledge now that we are inalienably forgiven; this makes it possible for us to be truly happy, since we are freed from that which of all things makes happiness impossible, which is fear. In so far as we are able to obey the command that we should love all men our happiness is yet further increased by the knowledge that all our fellow men, including all non-believers, are also forgiven and will be reconciled with God and united with him. We can only be compassionate about the fact that, because they do not know that they are forgiven, non-believers cannot share our happiness, and are constrained to live either in fear or in cynicism. And we must share guilt of the Church in that the notion of a vindictive God may frighten people into belief for a time but in the end will only encourage many men to prefer non-belief and despair.

We do not need therefore to fear the justice of God. There was no justice on Calvary, either in the condemnation of our Lord to death, or in the free salvation of a whole world lost in sin. Certainly, at the right time each one of us will have to face the truth about himself in the presence of his Lord; there can be no final reconciliation without truth. Certainly too in this life here and now, we must be honest with ourselves about our faults, be genuinely sorry for them and do our best to overcome them. But it makes all the difference that we do this for love, not from fear.

While Thomas spoke, apart from the time when he asked us the question about the woman in adultery, the whole village sat in silence, although I noticed that there were tears on the cheeks of many of the women and old men; this was only to be expected because Karpathians, for all their idiosyncrasies, are after all Greeks and therefore show their emotions more freely than we Romans. But when Thomas had finished speaking, the men could not contain themselves any longer and many of them stood up and shouted out words such as "Thomas is telling the truth!" "Christ has forgiven all men!" "God does not punish sinners!"

When the men had had their say, Thomas asked us to kneel and then all was quiet again while he said the prayers of confession and forgiveness, and led us in prayers for all our fellow men and women throughout the world.

Then the young people with him helped Thomas prepare the bread and wine for the Christian mystery, the Eucharist. He said the prayer of blessing of the bread and wine, with the very words which the Lord Jesus used to his disciples at the Last Supper, and prayed that the bread and wine should be for us, as it was for his friends then, the body and blood of the Lord himself. After that, when he and his young helpers were ready we all came forward down to the level space near the altar and knelt there, the mothers and fathers together with their children. Then Thomas moved among us with his helpers. The girls carried the bread, which he had broken into pieces after the prayer, and the boys carried the wine, still in the amphorae, which Thomas ladled out into the silver cup which one of the young people carried for him. As he came to each of us, Thomas put his hands on the heads of the children and called them by name and blessed them. He put a piece of bread in the hands of each of us adults, and called us by name and told us that the bread was the body of Christ; and when we had eaten it, he took the silver cup from the boy and gave it to us to drink from and told us it was the blood which the Christ had shed for the sins of the whole world.

When I took the bread and the wine I felt something I had never felt before, that I was at one with God; I knew that this was the ecstasy which the philosophers have written of, except that it came to me not on my own, but together with all the others there, in equality and union. And I understood with a sudden insight, though of course I did not put words to the thought until reflecting on it afterwards, that this faith has put an end for ever to the conflict between the reasoned humanism of the philosophers and the emotion of the mysteries, because in Jesus God became man and suffered, and because the Eucharist is for all men and women, equal before God because always and for ever children of God.

And now, although of course I want to be at home again and with my loved ones, yet at the same time I am loath to leave this place. Certainly I shall never come here again, and almost as certainly I shall not see Good Thomas again. For me, this is not an end, but a new beginning; I can indulge my regrets without serious hurt. But what will happen to him? Everything he has done here and all that he has stood for is so fragile, so vulnerable; even his personal peace and safety must be at risk. I can pray for him, but I am not sure what good that will do; while I have no doubt that God acts directly on our hearts and souls, my old sceptical distaste for superstition makes me doubt whether by praying we can alter any behaviour other than our own.

By the time I am home it may be that they will have brought your uncle Gaius back. Now that I am quite without doubt or fear for the welfare of my son's soul I can look forward to that encounter with equanimity.

Added while at Knidos on the voyage home:

We called in again here as we had on the way out, and have had to stay for two days while dangerous seas subside. My fears of unrest have proved only too well founded. While we were on Karpathos the Christians here have effected a violent and successful uprising. The temples of Aphrodite are being smashed down stone by stone and Praxiteles's masterpiece has been hammered to fragments; small compensation that there are copies in almost every city of the Empire! What has been devised for the priestesses and temple girls by way of 'punishment' (as this infamous form of public entertainment is called) I shall not describe: it is not seemly even to write or read of such things. The contrast with the story Thomas told us of Jesus and the woman who was about to be stoned makes me even more sure that my heresy is the truth.

10. PRIENE, December

My return home ten days ago was unexpectedly dramatic. I could sense at once that the embalmed body of your uncle Gaius had not yet reached the villa safely, even though it was now some three months after his death. I very soon had the explanation from one of Gaius's loyal former soldiers, who had been one of the escort for the coffin and had been sent on to us as a messenger to explain the prolonged delay. The journey has been little better than a nightmare. They have had to cross six provincial frontiers and at every one petty officials have invented some kind of tax which has to be paid to permit the transit of a corpse; in other words, they have demanded a bribe. Even now, the party was stranded near Nysa on the border crossing from Caria, with no money to meet the rapacious demands of the venial officials there. Naturally I did not delay in sending Mango and a fellow servant with a letter declaring my identity and my intention to report the matter to the provincial governor if the party were not immediately allowed to proceed without any further attempts at extortion.

Nor was that the only surprise awaiting me: there was another, of a very different kind. To my amazement I was greeted with great joy by your uncle-in-law Quintus, who had been with the family already for several days, recovering from the long and at times dangerous voyage from Gallaecia. The news, wonderful for all of us but above all for, your aunt Lucia and your cousins, is that he will from now on be stationed as close to us as could be, at Ephesos. While in Hispania he has become the best friend of a colleague whose uncle has just been appointed to the post of vicarius here; the uncle has invited his nephew to join his staff and there was no difficulty in arranging for Quintus to accompany him. The sad aspect of this is of course that, as soon as suitable accommodation in Ephesos can be had, Helvidia and I shall have to become used to our daughter and two of our granddaughters living no longer under our roof. But this is more than compensated by the joy that Quintus and his womenfolk will have in being able to be together again after nearly five years of such distant and unbroken separation, while their being as close to us as Ephesos is an astonishing stroke of good fortune.

Within only two days of my return the man whom I had sent with Mango to Nysa arrived back to say that all was well: the party with Gaius's body would arrive before nightfall; Mango had stayed with them to support Pyrrhos and make sure there were no other mishaps or impediments.

As the early dusk was gathering, the girls, having stayed all day on the look out, cried out that they could see the party approaching, and we all gathered by the main gate into the garden to greet them. They had the coffin in a horse-drawn cart which they brought right into the yard at the side of the villa. There the legionaries, six of them, halted and after saluting stayed near the cart some way from us. Pyrrhos and Mango came forward to where Helvidia and I were standing, and Pyrrhos fell on his knees while Mango stood at his side looking highly pleased with himself. I took Pyrrhos by the hand, raised him and thanked him from my heart for his loyalty and fortitude.

And there was yet another drama to unfold. In the background, near the soldiers but standing apart from them, was a young woman. She was simply dressed, slender and beautiful; her hair was dark but her complexion light and clear. Yet she was not a Greek - I guessed her at once to be a Persian. When I had finished speaking to Pyrrhos, she moved forward a few paces, and then stood waiting, modestly yet with her head not lowered. Unforeseen though her presence was to us, we all knew who she was: soldiers do not have a monopoly on loyalty.

There was nothing I could do but wait. For a few seconds, which seemed at the time much longer, no one of us moved. Then Helvidia went forward and embraced her. One could feel the tension passing off, and I remember thinking that in some ways at least we Romans should not make bad Christians. The girls then ran forward and took her by her hands and brought her to their mothers and then to me where she knelt and I kissed her hand and called her my daughter.

Her name is Parmys, and she speaks Greek quite well but no Latin. She lives with us now.

I then had to make the arrangements for Gaius's burial. Mango, knowing what would follow the obsequies, gained my permission to recruit among his fellow servants for a boar hunt. I wanted very much to have the bishop with us to give his blessing. So my first task was to ride over to Miletos to invite him. This was the first time I had seen Philip since I had heard of Gaius's death. He knew of course that I had been away, and understood that I had gone to be on my own in order to mourn my son; he did not know where I had been, nor did he ask, nor did I volunteer to tell him. We talked first of the project to build a church in Priene, and I congratulated him on what I had heard of Mark's reputation which was by all accounts benefiting from some mellowing of his speech and behaviour. I then put my request plainly to Philip, claiming the rights of friendship, keeping back my own intention of becoming a Christian (let alone what I had undergone on Karpathos) and not concealing the fact that Gaius had lived and died a pagan. For some time the bishop made no reply, but sat looking at me shrewdly over his hands clasped in front of him. Guessing his difficulty, I said: "My help for your church in Priene is not at issue; you have my promise for that already". Whereupon the old man rose from his chair beaming, clapped me on the shoulder and agreed to come and to give his blessing to my son.

We buried Gaius on a cold and bleak afternoon, in a grassy level place you will know well enough, a little up the hill, some three or four hundred paces from the villa. Mango had got the men to lay in the grave a simple stone sarcophagus which we had from the mason who is making the tombstone we shall set up late as soon as it is ready. The men laid Gaius down there; he was still in the cypress coffin in which they had brought him; it was open of course, so that we could put his tribune's cloak over him, and his sword by his side, and lay his right hand over his heart where they had shot him, and we could all see the gold ring on his finger. The girls had hunted far and wide to find some flowers for him, a few late yellow ground- lilies, some early snowdrops and narcissus. They laid a few of these in the coffin before the men closed and lowered it, and we then each threw a handful of earth into the grave, the soldiers and servants too. When the men had filled in the grave, the girls laid the rest of their flowers on the bare earth, the white and yellow petals bringing a welcome brightness to a scene gloomy enough otherwise. We had made a wooden cross to put at the head; I suspect that Mark, who came with Philip, disapproved of this, but the bishop himself seemed pleased. Against the cross we laid a wooden tablet on which Mango had branded the inscription I wanted:

**Gaius, son of Lucius, grandson of Aulus, Rutilius Rufus
Citizen of Rome
Child of God**

Then the bishop said a prayer for Gaius's soul, and I said something, a few words only, in praise of my son and gratitude to God for his life. In the spring we shall make a rose garden there.

The feast was the biggest affair we have had since we came here, and went on most of the night. We had to use the big barn, as I insisted on the servants eating with us. I wanted them to sit among us, but Helvidia told me not to be an old fool, because they would hate that. Of course she was right; we had one long table for us and three for them, with two for our tenants as well, and we all served each other in a disorganised way and everyone was happy. The girls tried to get Mark drunk; this was naughty of them, but their mothers did not intervene, which was also naughty. Their project was not altogether unsuccessful.

Another great pleasure for me has been to find your letters here waiting for me, and to know that you received the two I wrote on Karpathos. Forgive me for not having responded before (for the reason you know) to what you wrote some time ago about your father's provisions for your future. I hope you are content with the blessing which he has given in principle to your love for Myrto, and not therefore too disappointed with his decision that you must wait for a year at least before contemplating marriage. That Hermogenes is entirely in agreement with this does not surprise me; if you can excuse a repetition of the obvious, you are both exceedingly young.

I am of course delighted that your father wishes you to come back here for at least a part of the spring, in order to 'report' to me on all you have done and learnt during your year in Athens. I shall not, I promise, be too severe an examiner on academic matters or too inquisitive as to how your nights have been spent. I shall get great pleasure from sharing with you the experience which we now have in common of having been a student in Athens.

I welcome also most warmly Aulus's plan that you should spend the rest of next year in Rome, completing your studies and perfecting your Latin. The city once 'mistress of the world' is not I am afraid the intellectual centre it once was, while politically it grows less and less important almost by the day; the imperial family are only seriously interested these days in the new places, Milan, Trier, Nicomedia and so on (they say by the way that Byzantium has caught Constantine's eye). Yet there are still some professors worth hearing in Rome, and even more important is that you should have the experience simply of living there and getting to feel at home among all that is left of its former glories: it is still, you will find, a place of breathtaking beauty and unequalled majesty. Besides, you will I believe encounter one aspect of its life actually growing in importance, I mean its function as a centre of Christianity. I am told that the Christian basilicas which are rising up there now are quite the most magnificent in the Empire.

I am most interested to hear that Myrta has as her closest friend a girl who is Jewish and who adheres to the faith of her fathers. This makes me all the more glad that your parents and I have brought you up to have nothing to do with the hatred of Jewish people which can still be found even in good society among people who ought to know better. I fear too that this vice can be found among Christians, who in subjection to the incorrigible human lust for blame denigrate all Jews on the grounds that they were responsible for the crucifixion of the Christ. In fact the Roman as well as the Jewish authorities consented to his death, and it is obvious that the meaning of this is that it is not either the Jews or the Romans who are to be blamed, but the whole traditional notion of authority those involved represent, authority that is based on privilege and violence, and which survives by the exercise of these, precisely what it was an important part of Jesus's mission to subvert.

This reminds me of a conversation that I had with Thomas while I was on Karpathos and which I have not mentioned to you before. I asked him about that apparently extensive part of the Christian Bible which comprises the most important Jewish writings - neither Mango nor I have even begun to look at these yet. Thomas replied that they contain some profound allegories and that some of the early stories are both edifying and instinct with deep human feeling. There are also songs and poetry of the greatest beauty, expressing man's adoration for God in a fashion far beyond any of the expressions of Olympian religion or of the oriental mystics, and at least the equal of the most sublime passages of our greatest poets and philosophers. There is also a great deal of material concerned with the Jewish Law in all its elaboration, and of the history of the struggles of the Jewish people.

We discussed this, and agreed that, in view of what Jesus had to say about the legalities, the inclusion of Jewish Laws in all their meticulous detail within the Christians' most holy book was a curious anomaly. As for the history, stirring and full of high moral example as it often was, its purpose was to illuminate the story of a people who believed themselves to be specially chosen by God. It seemed hardly right that a chronicle whose whole purpose was so different both from the universal mission of the now virtually official Christian Church and from the cosmopolitan vision of the imperial authority should be ranked by that Church as equal in holiness to the account of the life and teaching of the Christian Lord himself and of his immediate followers.

Our conclusion was that the constitution of the Bible as it was could only be explained by the inevitable preoccupations of the first Christians in Palestine; their superstitious fascination with the whole subject of the so-called fulfilment of prophecy was a good example of this. Now that these preoccupations have long since ceased to be relevant to the Christian mission, and given the conflict between the whole thrust of Jewish history and the imperial interest, the present glorious revival of the fortunes of the Empire and policy for the universalisation of Christian membership should offer an ideal opportunity for setting this anomaly right. We envisaged the composition of a valuable handbook for Christian readers, having no pretension to rank in holiness with what I have learned to call the New Testament, which would bring together excerpts from the best writings of the Jewish patriarchs and prophets and of the Greek and Roman poets and philosophers. We should want to show too how it has not only been in the history of the Jewish people that God has revealed himself in a more direct way than through the inspired reasoning of the sages: can we not perceive the divine presence in the salvation of the Greeks at Marathon and Salamis, in the miraculous march to the sea of the Ten Thousand, in the lives of

Socrates, Epicurus and Seneca? In this way we should have a balanced presentation of the two great traditions out of which Christian thought has grown and in the light of which Christian experience has been interpreted.

Although I have not mentioned this idea yet to Bishop Philip, and have some apprehensions about how it will be received, I am considering the work of such a composition as a fitting task to occupy me during the next few years, while my faculties and Mango's are still unimpaired. I must first complete the treatise I am calling 'A Study of the Plants of Mycale', but (whatever your father and uncle have to say) I shall put off my idea of a history of the family since Publius Rutilius Rufus was consul in the year 649.

I shall not, it seems, be short of time for such a project: since I started dictating this for you, a letter has arrived with news which you no doubt have already received, and which will mean that our family here is soon to be even further reduced. But of course your grandmother and I rejoice for you, your mother and sisters at the news that your father will not be required to work again over the frontier in the foreseeable future, and that it is therefore safe for you all to join him in the peace and security of the provincial capital of Sardica.

We expect you here early next month, and so I shall not write to you again. Among the other letters that come from us with this, please give special attention to the one from me to Hermogenes to whom we all owe so much, and the private one from Helvidia for Myrto, the contents of which I have not seen but can presume to guess. The best arrangement is, as your father says, for you to stay with us here for a month or so and then escort your mother and sisters to New Dacia. You will then all be able to have some days together in your new home before you have to set out for Rome and your next adventure. You are indeed a young man to be envied.

If you are thinking of bringing anything home for us, I am told it is still possible to pick up quite good ancient vases in the Kerameikos without having to pay exorbitant prices. Something similar might do well for your parting gift for Hermogenes too; if I remember, he has a particular liking for black-figure.

Once you have left us, we shall be only three with the servants here, Helvidia, Parmys and I. The quiet will seem strange, especially in winter, when the road even to Ephesos can be too much for old bones. We shall miss the ladies and the girls dreadfully. Yet we have our own resources, and I cannot believe we shall be always dull.

What is more - it is a good principle to keep a sweet item until late in a letter - we shall not be reduced to two generations for long: I rejoice to tell you that Parmys is pregnant.

It is I suppose likely that when the festival of the Resurrection of the Christ comes next year we shall all be baptised publicly, I mean not only all the free ones and servants here (Mango and I keeping quiet about what we shared before) but also Quintus and Lucia and their children and servants too. That is of course if everyone is ready to make their commitment by then; somehow I think they will be.

That will be another opportunity for festivity to look forward to. And there is after all much to be thankful for. If only our great, heroic armies can keep our frontiers intact imagine that you - yes, and your children and grandchildren after you - will live to see the greatest days which our noble Empire and blessed civilisation have ever known, with the truth and goodness of the Christian faith acting as an all-powerful unifying force.

Meanwhile, nothing in life is more important to me than the knowledge, revived every time I and my womenfolk pay our daily visit to Gaius's grave, that his divine soul is safe for ever in union with the one, only, all-loving God.

Soon you will be sharing that daily visit with us, and by then there will be many more flowers for us to lay there.

Epilogue

ATHENS, January

Hermogenes to Lucius son of Aulus, cordial greetings.

When you have completed the rituals of welcome which are due to your grandson you will perhaps be able to find the time to read this letter which he has brought with him.

Your young Lucius has been a good pupil and a most delightful guest. Myrto will not be the only member of our little household to find that life is far less agreeable now that he has left us.

As one well experienced in bereavement I was able to share the depth of your sorrow at the loss of your son Gaius; that you have been able to come to terms with this is indeed a great blessing, one which it is not easy for me not to envy.

The love which my grandchild and yours have for each other is a source of much more than satisfaction to me. After the loss of my wife, my only child and her husband, all within a few days of each other, I had not supposed that I should ever experience the emotion of joy again. Thanks to our young people, and to the support of yourself and your noble son Aulus, my pessimism has been proved splendidly wrong.

By agreement with the two young people, it has been left to me to convey to you the results of our discussions in response to the Six Arguments you and Helvidia worked out in order to explain how and why it is that men have devised the notion that eternal punishment after death is the doom awaiting those who have earned the displeasure of the god.

First, let me say that we were all delighted with the six points you made; we particularly relished the distinction between what is right and what is good so neatly demonstrated in your last one. Naturally too we are, all three of us, entirely in agreement with your conclusion that the notion of eternal punishment is utterly unacceptable whether from a sceptical (notably, Epicurean) or religious (above all, Christian) point of view. Let us not forget that the idea of an ultimate resolution both of human suffering and human wrong-doing in a reconciliation with the Sovereign Good is to be found at the very foundation of our literature and so of our civilisation: I am thinking first and foremost of the transcending scene between Achilles and Priam which constitutes the fulfilment of Homer's Iliad, but also of the conclusions which Aeschylus finds for the curse of the House of Atreus and Sophocles for the tragedy of Oedipus.

We had no doubts either about the escalating process of cause and effect in this domain. Those who stand to benefit - the rich, the powerful, the holders of priestly office, those whom Thrasymachus in Plato's 'Republic' called "the stronger" invent the notion of a punishing god in order to justify in principle the operation of the punitive mechanisms they need in order to protect the unjust system by which they profit; once the notion of a punishing god becomes generally accepted by the very victims of the injustices, the practice of punishment by human authority has a ready-made and impregnable justification, enabling one hideous act of oppression to be heaped on another with impunity.

Moreover, it is not only their power which the powerful are able in this way to defend, but all the wickedness which goes with it: your Good Thomas was certainly right (we concluded) to point out how the stress on individual sin, and the horrendous penalties which it is said to incur, can operate as excellent cover for every kind of despotic excess.

I noticed by the way that in the reference in one of your letters to those who were subjected to eternal punishment in Hades according to the traditional Greek mythology, there was one notable instance which escaped your memory: you made no mention of Prometheus, condemned for ever to have his bowels torn by a vulture for having stolen fire from the gods in order to give it to mankind. You missed here a perfect illustration of one of your own insights, that a principal function of hell is to protect authority from the rebel, no matter how enlightened.

Much as we admire your arguments, we believe however that we can adduce stronger proofs of the actual impossibility of eternal divine punishment than seem to have occurred to you, at least as far as is revealed in your series of letters.

We have three of these which we consider to be valid for all those who believe in the Sovereign Good (and without that belief there can be no foundation for the notion of divine justice anyway). All relate to the question of what is a possible and what is an impossible relationship between the temporal and eternal worlds - the worlds in Platonic terms of 'happening' and 'being'. Now of course the possibility of there being any such relationship is a mystery, and I for one would not for a single moment pretend to understand how it works; not being a Christian I am not able to emulate Alexander by 'cutting the Gordian knot' as you and Myrto can by means of what you call the 'Incarnation'. It is obvious that since we are only conscious of what it is like to live in the temporal world, our understanding of the eternal one is necessarily extremely limited. All the same, I am confident that we can identify certain relations between the temporal and the eternal which are simply not possible. I believe in the notion of progress, as far as it concerns man's understanding of the world; the elimination of impossible theories is one important way in which progress can be made.

Of our three proofs, one derives essentially from the nature of the eternal and one more evidently from the nature of the temporal, while the third is centred on an essential aspect of the relation between them.

Since a belief in the Sovereign Good excludes a Zoroastrian solution to the problem of Good and Evil, we must believe that only the Good is eternal; Evil is contingent, and exists only in the temporal world. But since too the only good attitude towards the god on the part of any soul is that of love (a yearning for union), and the only good condition of any soul is that of union, the notion of souls eternally suffering, unable to love the god and forever out of union with the god, would require the eternal existence of that which is evil, which is impossible.

Secondly, to take next the proof based on an essential relation between the temporal and the eternal, the only possible ultimate cause of all things temporal is the eternal (again, the god). It is the nature of the eternal to cause the temporal, for the temporal to be the effect of the eternal. The notion of a temporal condition or set of behaviours having an eternal effect is therefore an absurdity.

Our final proof, the one which starts rather from the nature of the temporal world, is a moral one and will need a slightly longer exposition. We start from the assumption that a good god cannot be unjust; we then demonstrate that the eternal punishment of any soul which has inhabited a body in the temporal world could not be anything but unjust.

The reason for this is that human life is systematically subject to chance and accident. There is the accident of the personal qualities which we inherit from our ancestors and with which we are born; there is the accident of our upbringing and the influences, which must be powerful and may be effectively irresistible, to which we are subjected during our tender years; there is the accident of all the eventualities, good and bad, which impinge on a man's life, including the time and manner of his death.

The important consequence is that men are never totally responsible and never totally not responsible for whatever they do. And it follows from this that the condemnation of a soul either to death or to eternal punishment could not in any single case be just. (You remember how I used to argue - something I still believe that among men, given the systematic relativity of responsibility, and given that in all cases some element of provocation, external influence or derangement will apply, a death penalty for whatever crime is always unjust; even in the cases of the most horrific crimes, when we believe that the act is so horrible that it must deserve death, it is the absolute quality of the act we have in mind, the relativity of the agent's responsibility is not affected by the level of awfulness of the crime; and in so far as we believe that death is necessary in order to protect society from the culprit's future crimes, that is not as such a punishment, more like a kind of war against the individual).

I invited Myrto and your young namesake to devise examples in support of this third proof of ours. Myrto instanced a girl brought up in a devout Christian family; at her father's insistence she does not marry, but devotes her life to caring for him after her mother's death; on his death bed, he arranges for her to be taken into the house of a group of holy women, and there she spends the rest of her life in prayer and good works until she dies a virgin who has never once walked down the street or been seen in a public place. With that Myrto contrasted the life of a boy born to live in a band of brigands, ultimately suffering a violent death after a career devoted to the pillage, rape, injury and murder of his fellow men and women; illiterate, he has only ever learned the names of the gods as material for his curses. One of these lives a life of near sanctity and the other one of effective satanism; neither has ever had the choice to be other than they are.

Your Lucius, developing Myrta's idea, imagined two men brought up together like her brigand and operating for a number of years as partners in a series of crimes of barbarous cruelty. They are attacked and overpowered by a rival gang, and one of the two is killed. The other escapes though badly wounded. He finds his way to a cottage where his wounds are tended; he recovers and lives to an advanced age, but permanently crippled and dependent. The woman who has nursed him is a Christian; she devotes her life to his care, and under her influence he repents. The first of the two former fellow criminals spends eternity in hell, the second in heaven. Where is the justice of the god?

At this point we found that we could imagine two possible objections which needed to be countered. The first is that our examples consist of extreme experiences, and it is universally recognised that you cannot make a rule out of exceptional cases. Moreover the god, as well as being good and just, is both infinitely knowing and infinitely wise; no aspect of what is relevant to each case will escape him and his capacity to make correct judgments is by definition incapable of error. Our response to this objection is that our examples, though dramatic in character in order to highlight the issues, are not in the least exceptional in essence; on the contrary, to be subject to accident, and therefore never more (nor less) than partially responsible for our actions is the inescapable lot of all men and women at all times. That either the death or eternal punishment of any human soul could ever be just is therefore categorically impossible; to this a recognition of the god's omniscience and boundless wisdom is simply irrelevant.

The second objection takes this form: it is not for us mere men to impugn the justice of the god. Since everything the god does is by definition holy, every act he performs is self-justifying and any suggestion that in punishing sinners the god could be acting unjustly would itself be a grave sin worthy of divine anger and punishment. Myrto tells me that this view is commonly held by her fellow Christians; indeed she has the impression that a belief in the unassailable righteousness of the god's anger and the irrelevance to this of merely human ideas about justice is required Christian orthodoxy, not to adhere to it being a dire heresy.

You will I believe forgive me, my dear Lucius, if I say that in my opinion such a view is logically untenable, empirically refutable, morally malignant and spiritually blasphemous; I believe this because I am confident that you share my views on this. What we know for certain is that the god has given mankind a clear, sure and inviolable perception of the fundamental difference between good and evil; if we deny that we deny all philosophy, we are nihilists with nothing to discuss. Our feeling for justice is either a revelation of the nature of the justice of the god, or the Good is not Sovereign. What we mean when we say that the god is good and just (let alone, as you Christians say, that he 'is love') cannot fail to be a true reflection of what we normally and naturally mean by these words, for the simple reason that our knowledge of goodness and justice (and, for Christians, of love also) is derived solely and entirely from the god; otherwise again our belief in the Sovereignty of the Good would be meaningless.

The alternative, that the retribution of the god demands our acceptance whether or not it corresponds to our idea of justice (an idea which is either god-given or empty of meaning) is merely barbaric. It would imply that the god is to be worshipped not because he is good but merely because he is powerful; we might as well worship Moloch or the demons imagined by ignorant and indigent wretches. Yet we can see at once how popular this abominable conception is and will always be with despots, who will do everything in their power to propagate it, in combination with the dubious doctrine that their own authority derives directly from the god: if the justice of the god is once allowed to be arbitrary, then there is no limit set to the excesses which they can indulge in the name of justice in order to escalate and perpetuate their own 'god-given' tyrannies.

Myrto, I am happy to say, is in complete agreement with me and your grandson over this. I believe too that she is coming round to my point of view on another question which greatly exercises the minds of the group of young Christians of which she is a member. Their problem is that they are called to believe that loving the god is something that we can freely choose to do or not to do, whereas since the god is not liable to the bonds of time he knows in advance the whole of what is to us the future, including all the choices that will ever be made to love him or no; all such choices are therefore predetermined and the notion that they are freely made is consequently an illusion. I have insisted that it is the problem, not the freedom, which is illusory, since it depends on a total failure to reflect on what little we can be sure of concerning what it is like to be 'in eternity'. It is clearly childish to suppose that being outside time is in all respects the same as being within it except for the ability to see the future. We may, for want of better words, speak of the god seeing what is for us the future; to speak of his doing this 'in advance' is utterly without meaning. The reality must be that the god's knowledge of what is to us in the future no more determines what that will be than does the god's or indeed our knowledge of what has happened in what is to us the past predetermine that.

I find myself compelled to conclude that much of what causes confusion and distress in all these questions is due to failure of the intellect, either as a result of a lack of mental capacity or to indolence in its use. To that extent, there may after all be much in what Socrates had to say about the dependence of virtue on knowledge.

Yet there is for sure a great deal more excuse for uncertainty, and consequent distress, on the issue of the immortality of the soul itself. Unlike you, I have never, as you know, been attracted by the Epicurean insistence on the dispersal of the soul at death. The idea that the soul pertains to the divine seems to me more probable than any alternative, though goodness knows I have no means of proving this. What on the other hand seems to me evidently absurd is the commonplace belief that our individual souls will exist for ever even though they came into existence for the first time at the moment of our physical birth - as if anything merely temporal in its origin could after a period of existence in time become a part of the eternal. If our souls are, in any sense or mode, to live for ever, they must have lived for ever, and must be living for ever now; this is surely so obvious that any child could understand it and perceive its irresistible truth. The commendable element in the otherwise superstitious beliefs of the Orphists and others who adhere to the doctrine of the transmigration of souls is simply this, that they encourage us to look back at the life of our souls as well as forwards. Has it occurred to you what is the defect in Plato's 'myth' that before our physical birth we have to drink the waters of forgetfulness from the river Lethe? It is that he supposed that what we forget then is merely our knowledge of the past, whereas the truth must be that we forget also our knowledge of the future, which our souls naturally possess as pertaining to the divine.

Myrto likes to speak of us as made in 'the image of God', while for me a better metaphor is that our souls are fragments of the god, which come from the god and can only return to the god. A great merit of this view is that it offers a satisfactory explanation of why it is that our souls yearn for the god, and continue to do so in spite of all the doubts that assail us even about his very existence.

When both my oldest friend and my only grandchild have made the same philosophic choice, I have naturally had to consider whether to follow their example. I suspect you will not be surprised and hope you will not be grieved when I say that I have decided not to do this.

The preference for an eclectic position which we shared as young men is something which still seems to come naturally to me: I like to pick and choose the elements that appeal to me from all the prominent Schools and creeds rather than commit my allegiance to anyone. This is partly because I find on rational examination that the remedies offered by no one system amount to a panacea: 'virtue is knowledge' , but not only that; 'everything flows' is valid for one aspect of reality, of which stability is another; the right choice can be found 'in a golden mean between extremes', but not always; 'know thyself' is a necessary but insufficient principle on which to base our daily lives; and so on. Besides, I am by temperament not a good joiner of societies or sects of any kind. You are no doubt right in deciding that if one is to be a Christian then one must accept the responsibility of being a member of the association which Christians call their 'Church' , and a good, active member at that. I cannot by any means imagine myself as a Church person.

There are, I must confess, more weighty considerations. It is difficult for me not to be put off by the large place afforded in your Evangels to miraculous performances. Astonishing acts of healing hardly trouble me: all of us have heard of such things on good authority, and may have had direct experience of them in one form or another. Besides, it is obvious that our knowledge of what can be achieved by healing skills is in its infancy. Natural miracles however, such as walking on water, calming a storm, multiplying a meagre supply of food, smack of sensational superstition; to allow myself a feeble pleasantry, I find wine made out of water hard to swallow. Then again the notion of sacrifice which, if I understand Myrto rightly, is essential to the significance of the Christ's execution, would from a philosophic point of view take us back rather than forward. And then there is the crowning miracle, what you call the 'resurrection' ; without a belief in this, so your Paul of Tarsus says, there simply is no Christian faith at all. You can see that this creates problems for me.

It is of course a source of critical relief to me that both Myrto and you are believers in the universality of the 'salvation' which it was the mission of the Christ to deliver; I say 'critical' because the thought that either of you could adhere to a doctrine either of the punitive death of aberrant souls or of their eternal punishment would both cause me the most acute distress and erect an insurmountable moral barrier between us. Happily, for Myrto, as for you, the issue is clear cut: since those who believe in Christ are 'called' to this by the holy spirit of the god, since therefore (in the terms you used in one of your earlier letters) 'grace' precedes 'faith', she asserts with conviction that the idea of death or eternal punishment for those who are not so called is formally and decisively incompatible with that of the goodness of the god. I have to say that this seems to me so obvious that anyone would have to be exceedingly stupid or profoundly wicked to deny it. Yet, the reality is that the great majority of Christians believe in hell, not to believe it being (so you all tell me) explicitly designated an unforgivable heresy. I respect the decision that you and Myrto are making, which is to deal with the dilemma of either being a member or a heretic by ignoring it and cheerfully (as it were) proceeding to be both at once; you will perhaps see that I would find the mental gymnastics which that involves more than I can manage.

My dear old friend, do not be offended by what I have said

here. The points I have made are not put before you as arguments: to argue on questions such as these is both discourteous and fruitless. My intention has been no more than to communicate to you in the spirit of candour which was such an essential part of our converse and friendship in the old days. I want you to understand my position, because I need very badly that you should respect it, as I promise to respect yours. The real difference between us is not that I am more sceptical and you more credulous, or anything of that sort; it is simply that I have not had the same experiences that you have. My bereavements, unlike your loss of Gaius, did not happen at a time when I was deeply engaged in re-examining my beliefs about the future of our souls in the context of a newly accelerated impact of the Christian reality. And, even more to the point, I have not met your Good Thomas.

Once your grandson has taken my Myrto from me, I shall be faced with an even quieter and more solitary life than you. But not for so long, I suspect: there are signs that my health is declining. No doubt you will want the marriage to take place on your side of the water. If we can agree to delay it until the spring after next, when the Aegean will be in a good enough mood for an old man to venture on it, may I take it that I am invited? I am prepared to brave the wild boars and lynxes of the wilderness on the edge of which you have chosen to live, provided you promise not to try to convert me either to Christianity or to sea-bathing. Of these, you will never convince me that the second at least is a fit activity for a gentleman accustomed to life in a civilised metropolis.

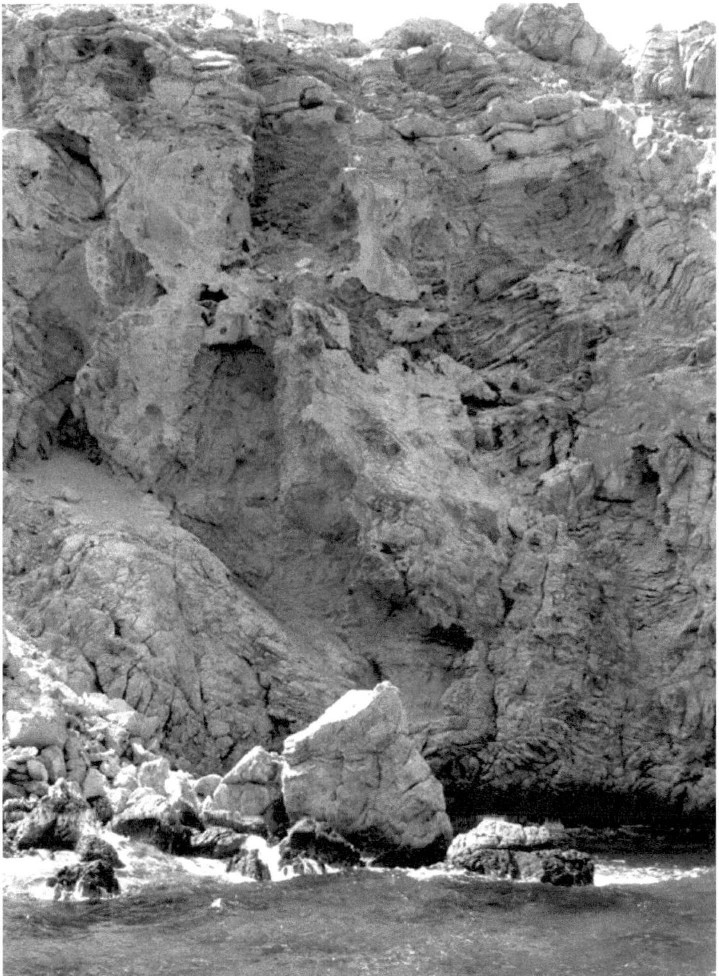

Geographical Names and Terms

Aegina: island in the Saronic Gulf between Attica and the isthmus; once a considerable naval power, distinguished for gallantry at the battle of Salamis against the Persian invaders.

Ancyra: now Ankara.

Aphrodisias: noted as a centre for the worship of Aphrodite (the Roman Venus), goddess of physical love and another of the twelve great gods. There are impressive remains of her precinct; her temple was later converted into a church.

Armenia: the Roman province forming the frontier with Persia.

Attic manner: Attica being the region in which Athens lies.

Byzantium: shortly after these Letters were written, Constantine launched his project to move the capital of the Empire here from Rome, with the new name of Constantinople.

Caria: Priene was in the Province of Asia; Caria was the next Province to the south. The **Carians** occupied this part of the coast and towards the south before the arrival of the Ionian colonists.

Corcyra: now Corfu.

Corinth: in spite of its inclusion here, retained some of its wealth into imperial times.

Dorian allies: the Dorians, one of the three chief tribes of the Greeks, occupied the southern and western parts of the Greek mainland, and the southern parts of the Aegean islands and Asian coastline.

Ephesos: was the chief city of the Asiana Dioecesis, comprising ten provinces, including Asia and Caria.

Euxine: the Black Sea.

Gallaecia: corresponds to present Galicia, in north west Spain.

Hierapolis: a celebrated spa; now Pamukkale, still visited for its waters.

Lesbos: chief island of the Aeolian Greeks, who colonised the northern section of the coast of Asia Minor

Kos and Knidos: Greek cities of the south-west coast of Asia Minor (Turkey).

Maeander river: origin of the word 'meander'; now the Menderes.

Marathon and Salamis: sites of decisive Greek victories over the Persian invaders in 490 and 480 B.C.

Marcomannia: in south central Germany, beyond the frontier of the Empire.

Megara: on the isthmus of Corinth; once a flourishing city, responsible for the founding of Byzantium.

Melos: island of the Cyclades, now Milos.

Mycale: the headland on the south of which Priene lay; now Samsun.

New Dacia, Sardica: Dacia proper was north of the Danube, roughly corresponding to south central Romania. When in the third century the Romans abandoned it to the Goths, a province of 'New Dacia' was created out of part of the old province of Moesia, south of the river. Sardica is Sofia.

Nicaea: now Isnik, in north west Asia Minor (Turkey); the first Ecumenical Council took place here in 325.

Nicomedia: on the opposite coast of Propontis (Sea of Marmara) from Byzantium, and chief city of the Dioecesis of Pontus.

Panionium: the cooperative union of the twelve cities ('dodecapolis') of the Ionians; as well as Priene, member cities mentioned in the letters were Miletos, Ephesos and Phocaea. The Ionian colonists from central Greece occupied the islands in the middle of the Aegean and the central part of the western coastline of Asia Minor (Turkey) in the ninth century B.C.

Peiraeus: still the port of Athens.

Pergamum: once capital of an independent kingdom, still celebrated at the time of these Letters for its library and as a centre of healing.

Phocaea: one of the twelve Greek cities of Ionia; played a leading part in the colonising enterprise.

Poseideion: the chief town of the island, now known as Pigadia or simply Karpathos

Priene: small but ancient city of the Ionian Greeks, on the west coast of Asia Minor (now Turkey), between Ephesos and Miletos.

Seven Provinces: these covered most of southern Gaul (France).

Stageirite: Aristotle was born in 384 B.C at Stageira in north western Greece.

Temple of Zeus: completed in 132 A.D; substantial remains have survived.

Guide to Classical Names, Terms and References

Achilles and Priam: a reconciliation between the Greek hero Achilles and Priam, king of Troy, whose son Hector he had killed, takes place in the last book of Homer's Iliad.

Aeschylus: his tragic trilogy (the 'Orestieia') was first produced in Athens in 458 B.C.; it ends with the redemption of the hero Orestes.

Alexander, the Great King: Alexander of Macedon finally defeated Darius, King of Persia, and put an end to the Persian Empire, in 331 B.C.

Amasis: philhellene ruler of Egypt, sixth century B.C.

Antigone: Sophocles's 'Antigone' was first produced in Athens in or about 441 B.C.

Apollo (Phoebus) and Artemis: brother and sister, associated respectively with the sun and the moon, the Roman Apollo and Diana; were among the great gods. Apollo, who was also god of prophecy and music, had his most important shrine at Delphi in central Greece, where his priest operated the celebrated oracle.

Aristophanes: writer of satirical and farcical comedies in the fifth century 'golden age' of Athens.

Aristotle's 'Ethics' : Aristotle founded what came to be known as the Peripatetic School of philosophy and natural science in Athens about the middle of the fourth century B.C.

Arius: at this time excommunicated and in exile, but his influence was still very great; he died about 336.

Asclepius: god of medicine and healing, the Roman Aesculapius.

Athene the Guardian: the Roman Minerva and another of the twelve great gods, was the patron goddess of Priene; substantial remains of her temple there survive.

Aurelian: Emperor 270-275.

Cato (the Elder) : Roman consul in 195 and censor in 184 B.C.

Caracalla: Emperor 212-217.

Catullus: leading Roman poet of the first century B.C; the words "I love and hate" are the start of an epigram on the torments of sexual love.

Clement: Christian 'father' and head of the Catechetical School of Alexandria in the second century.

Cicero: leading exponent of Roman oratory, and conservative statesman; assassinated by order of Mark Antony in 43 B.C.

Crispus: Constantine's eldest son; a 'Caesar' at this time was a kind of assistant Emperor, with expectations for succession; the Emperor himself carried the title Augustus.

Decius: Emperor 249-251.

Demeter: goddess of corn, equated with the Roman Ceres; one of the twelve great gods.

Diocletian: Emperor 284-305, he reorganised the Empire, but his great reign was marred by a revival of the Christian persecution.

Epicurean: follower of the materialist philosopher Epicurus, who founded his School in Athens towards the end of the fourth century B.C.

Eusebius: leading Christian scholar and historian, of Caesarea in Palestine; active at the time of these Letters.

Exekias: Athenian potter and vase painter, working in black-figure in the sixth century B.C.

Galerius: Emperor 293-310.

Gallienus: he reigned as Augustus 253-267

Georgic: Virgil's four books of Georgics describe in verse the practice of farming in Italy in his day.

Hades (also Dis and Pluto): was brother of Zeus and Poseidon and lord of the underworld.

Hadrian: he ruled 117-138.

Hera: the Roman Juno, wife of Zeus (Jupiter) and queen of the gods.

Heraclitus: philosopher living about 500 B.C.

Herodotus: 'Father of History'; historian of the Greco-Persian wars, fifth century B.C.

Leading philosopher: Alexander, succeeded as archbishop of Alexandria by Athanasius four years after these letters were written.

Lethe: traditionally one of the rivers of hell.

Longinus: professor of literature in Athens in the third century A.D; traditionally the celebrated literary treatise 'On the Sublime' was attributed to him.

Lucian: author of Dialogues of comment and criticism, written in Greek in the second century A.D.

Lucretius: expounded the philosophy of Epicurus (see note for page 21) in a Latin poem entitled 'On the Nature of the World', written in the first century B.C.

Lysias and Isocrates: Athenian orators of the best period, fifth and fourth centuries B.C.

Menander: writer of comedies of manners in Athens, fourth century B.C.

Mithras and Isis: of respectively Persian and Egyptian origin, their cults were immensely popular.

Olympian religion: the traditional worship of the twelve great gods, imagined as living on Mount Olympus in northeast Greece.

Origen: Christian scholar and theologian, taught and wrote in Alexandria and in Caesarea, Palestine, during the first half of the third century.

Orphic cult: a religious movement, traditionally founded by the semi-mythical Thracian singer Orpheus; it included a belief in the transmigration of souls.

Ovid: elegiac poet in the time of Augustus, was exiled in 8 A.D to Tomis (now Constanta) on the Black Sea near the mouth of the Danube.

Periclean Athens: a 'golden age', during the leadership of the democratic politician Pericles, middle of the fifth century B.C.

Phocylides: writer of epigrams in verse, sixth century B.C.

Plato's Republic: written in Athens in the first half of the fourth century B.C, this, the most celebrated of all the works of the philosopher Plato, describes the constitution of the ideal state, governed by 'philosopher kings'.

Pliny (the Elder) : author of a voluminous Natural History in the first century A.D; killed by the eruption of Vesuvius in 79.

Plotinus: head of the New Academy (i.e. Platonic School), taught in Alexandria and Rome in the third century A.D.

Polybius: Greek historian of Rome, second century B.C.

Plutarch: philosopher and biographer of the latter part of the first century A.D, he wrote in Greek a collection of some fifty lives of leading Greek and Roman persons, of which that of Alexander the Great is one.

Poseidon: god of the sea, the Roman Neptune; another of the twelve great gods.

Praxiteles: leading sculptor, working in the middle of the fourth century B.C. The best Roman copy of the Aphrodite of Cnidus is in the Vatican; a fragment in the British Museum may be original.

Prometheus: his tragedy forms one of the later dramatic works of Aeschylus, produced in Athens probably in the 450s B.C.

Protagoras: professional sophist, practising in Athens during the fifth century B.C.

Proteus: a mythical person with the gift of prophecy and capacity to change his shape at will.

Pythagoreans: followers of Pythagoras, mathematician and philosopher of the sixth century B.C.

Sassanid: this dynasty established the New Persian Empire in 224 A.D and ruled for over four hundred years.

Seneca: Stoic philosopher, writer and tutor of Nero, in Rome in the first century A.D.

Servius Sulpicius: Stoic Roman aristocrat of the latter days of the Republic, first century B.C.

Socrates: was executed 'for corrupting the youth' by means of hemlock poison in 399 B.C.

Sophocles: the last of the Oedipus plays, in which the hero is reconciled to his fate, was 'Oedipus at Colonus' first produced at Athens in 401 B.C., several years after the playwright's death at the age of ninety.

Stoic: follower of Zeno, who taught in the Stoa Poikile (Painted Hall) in Athens in the fourth century B.C.

Ten Thousand: heroic retreat of Greek mercenaries from inland Persia to the sea in 399 B.C, recorded some years after the event by the Athenian historian Xenophon.

Terence: Roman writer of comedies based on Greek models, second century B.C.

Theophrastus: second head of the Peripatetic School of philosophy founded in Athens by Aristotle in the fourth century B.C, and author of a celebrated 'History of Plants'.

Thrasymachus: philospher and rhetorician, practising in Athens at the end of the fourth century B.C.

Thucydides: Athenian historian of the war between Athens and Sparta, latter part of the fifth century B.C.

Tiberius Gracchus: Roman consul in 177 and 163 B.C.

Titus: he captured Jerusalem in 70.

Victories of Constantine: culminating in the final overthrow of his rival Licinius in 323, and thus uniting the Empire.

Year 649; that is, from the Foundation of the City of Rome: 105 B.C.

Zeus: the sky god and king of the gods, the Roman Jupiter.

Zoroastrian: the Persian religion, founded by Zoroaster, perhaps in the tenth century B.C.

Zoroastrian solution: both good and evil are conceived as eternal and engaged in combat forever.

A NOTE ON THE TEXT

Ten Letters To A Grandson was first printed privately by my father in September 1996. A small number of the A4, spiral-bound manuscripts was circulated to immediate family and friends but there is no evidence that any attempts were made to contact publishers.

There were always *eleven* Letters, but in July 2002 Dad produced in the same format a longer work - *The Mango Papers* - which opens with the *Ten Letters ...* largely unchanged. Yet this is a very different text, with a Foreword and General Introduction that suggest an impatience with the original concept of a trove of discovered papers. Here, the Letters are followed by three 'Gospel Dialogues' transcribed by Mango from conversations between him and his master, Lucius. Finally, in a section called 'The Gospels of Life and Death' Mango combines a brief further narrative with five sets of notes by Thomas of Karpathos "which set out a highly innovatory, not to say heretical conflation of the Four Gospels".

But to remain with the original manuscript of *Ten Letters* ... is to find a purer thing: a self-contained, distinctive moment in Christian history, set against a lifetime of personal reflections. Within this text, there are particular Christian debates which fascinated my father, not least the belief in universal salvation, and the exploration of one 'true' Gospel text. *The Mango Papers* develop further these preoccupations, while losing some of the narrative authenticity and harmony of the original Letters. The spirit of the Papers' new material was revisited and expanded upon in Dad's final (and as yet unfinished) project *Good Gospel Good God*.

So, as an entity, the Letters make a more striking and coherent read, especially because of their playful pretence of validity, which was diluted by later inceptions. Tinged with tragedy, these missives present a compassionate, expansive picture of what the early Christian Church offered to an enlightened outsider. At the same time, schismatic shadows and mob violence touch the edges of Lucius' story. The introduction concludes by saying that:

> [Lucius'] family name does not appear among those of the landowners within the Asian provinces in any indexed text of the Byzantine period.

We are left to fear the worst for the Letters' author, and his people.

There is a further dimension to the Letters: how they echo Dad's other preoccupations and circumstances. In 1996, he was a seventy-one year old grandfather, retired for a few years in the new and pleasant environment of south Cambridgeshire. It was a golden time for my mother Jean, and him. Like Lucius, he had four grown up children, a daughter and three sons, and, like his Roman counterpart, he had (at that point) five grandchildren, distributed across the second generation in the same way as in the Letters. Then, his only grandson was just eight years old. The expanding family was at the centre of my parents' lives.

Dad had been drawn to writing for much of his career, as shown by the seminal educational text, *Comprehensive Values*[1] and his two books on provision for the disabled[2]. He produced several

---

[1] Heinemann, 1975
[2] *Meeting Disability* (Cassell, 1991) and, with Peter Mittler, *Teacher Education for Special Needs in Europe* (Cassell, 1995).

other significant and (so far) unpublished works in retirement. A personal memoir[3] and an extraordinarily thorough family genealogy[4] were followed by two theological explorations: *Two Thousand Years Of Wrong*[5] and *Good Gospel, Good God*[6]. Like Lucius, he found perspective and enormous creative drive, in his more mature years.

Before all of that, Dad was a classicist, academic and teacher. He returned to that first vocation in retirement, teaching the Classics to adults. And, just as Lucius has recently retired from an office of empire, Dad had left Brussels and his work in the European Commission a few years before writing the Letters. That sense of a an imperfect but fondly-remembered world order permeates Lucius's writing.

Dad was a very knowledgeable amateur botanist, and founded his village's Nature Watch group. His work in Romania left him with a particular love of that country, and its people, as illustrated by the Letters' academic connection with Cluj and the descriptions of Old Dacia.

Lacking Lucius' over-patriarchal attitude towards women, Dad did perhaps share the benevolent envy of his narrator for the remembered opportunities of youth. Does his grandson appreciate them? That French saying "si jeunesse savait, si vieillesse pouvait"[7] was one of Dad's favourites, and could be applied equally to the young Lucius' opportunities in learning, and love.

Yet Dad, like that other grandfather, was energised by the opportunities of his age, and as fearless in his travels as he was in his strategies for persuading my mother to journey with him.

A few of *The Mango Papers*' amendments to the Letters have been included in this text. "Mad John" on Karpathos becomes "Mad Thomas", or simply "Thomas". This adjustment prevents confusion with the references to John the Apostle, or Divine. Additionally, I have included Chapter 9's paragraph beginning "We do not need therefore to fear the justice of God" (on pages 93-94); likewise, the

---

[3] *A Comedy of Faith*.
[4] *Roots and Branches: Towards a History of the Family of Daunt*. See p. 103!
[5] Completed in ... 2000.
[6] This was first completed in 2009, but Dad was working on an extensive revision of the text in the last year of his life.
[7] "If youth knew; if old age could".

second sentence on p. 84 is new. Such additions no doubt underline some of the themes upon which *The Mango Papers* expand.

The Letters' original notes have been re-ordered for convenience and a sub-heading or two have been added. Contextual photographs - that have been placed outside the main text - were taken in the eastern Aegean in September 2019.

I am very grateful to Jonathan Clatworthy for his encouragement of this project. Jonathan is a Trustee of Modern Church (https://modernchurch.org.uk/), an organization which was dear to the heart of Pat Daunt.

Will Daunt   **November 2019**